What Others are Saying:

This is a much-needed guide relevant at every level of government. It sets out what every public servant needs to know about open government and transparency, whether elected, appointed, or hired, and serves as a reminder that our task is to represent the often-forgotten taxpayer! It should be required reading for civil servants and elected representatives and all who desire to preserve the public trust.

–Andrea Seastrand, Former California Assembly Member,
Former Representative, US House of Representatives

Public Integrity is the foundation for citizen faith in local government. Elected and appointed officeholders hijacking official authority to benefit themselves and their cronies, or to punish those who expose their corruption, jackhammers away those foundations. Debbie Peterson's guide on how to spot, avoid, and remedy corrupt practices from the inside by local elected and appointed officeholders is indispensable for every city council and agency board member.

–Stew Jenkins, Constitutional Attorney, Former Harbor Commissioner

Debbie Peterson knows the rules that govern elected and appointed officials' public behavior. This new book defines those rules, so even the most minor official can serve with confidence, knowing how to stay transparent, honest and avoid any appearance of impropriety, while always honoring the public trust!

–Peter Keith, Former Mayor, GROVER BEACH, CALIFORNIA

CITY COUNCIL 101

CITY COUNCIL 101

Insider's Guide for New Councilmembers

by former **Mayor Debbie Peterson**

For more information or to contact the author, visit www.DebbiePeterson.com

paperback ISBN: 979-8-9862195-3-0
hardcover ISBN: 979-8-9862195-4-7
eBook ISBN: 979-8-9862195-5-4

Printed in the United States of America

Contact info:
Info@DebbiePeterson.com
www.DebbiePeterson.com

GOOD NEWS!—You do not have to read this book from start to finish. If you are running for office or already serving you may not have time to do additional reading. Simply read what you need to know now and read the rest later. The principles here apply to local government everywhere. You don't have to be newly elected, and you don't have to be a Councilmember. Other local government representatives, staff members, and interested citizens will also find it helpful. Even seasoned representatives will find wisdom here that will serve them. This book is meant to be a handbook, a guide, an inspiration, a prompt.

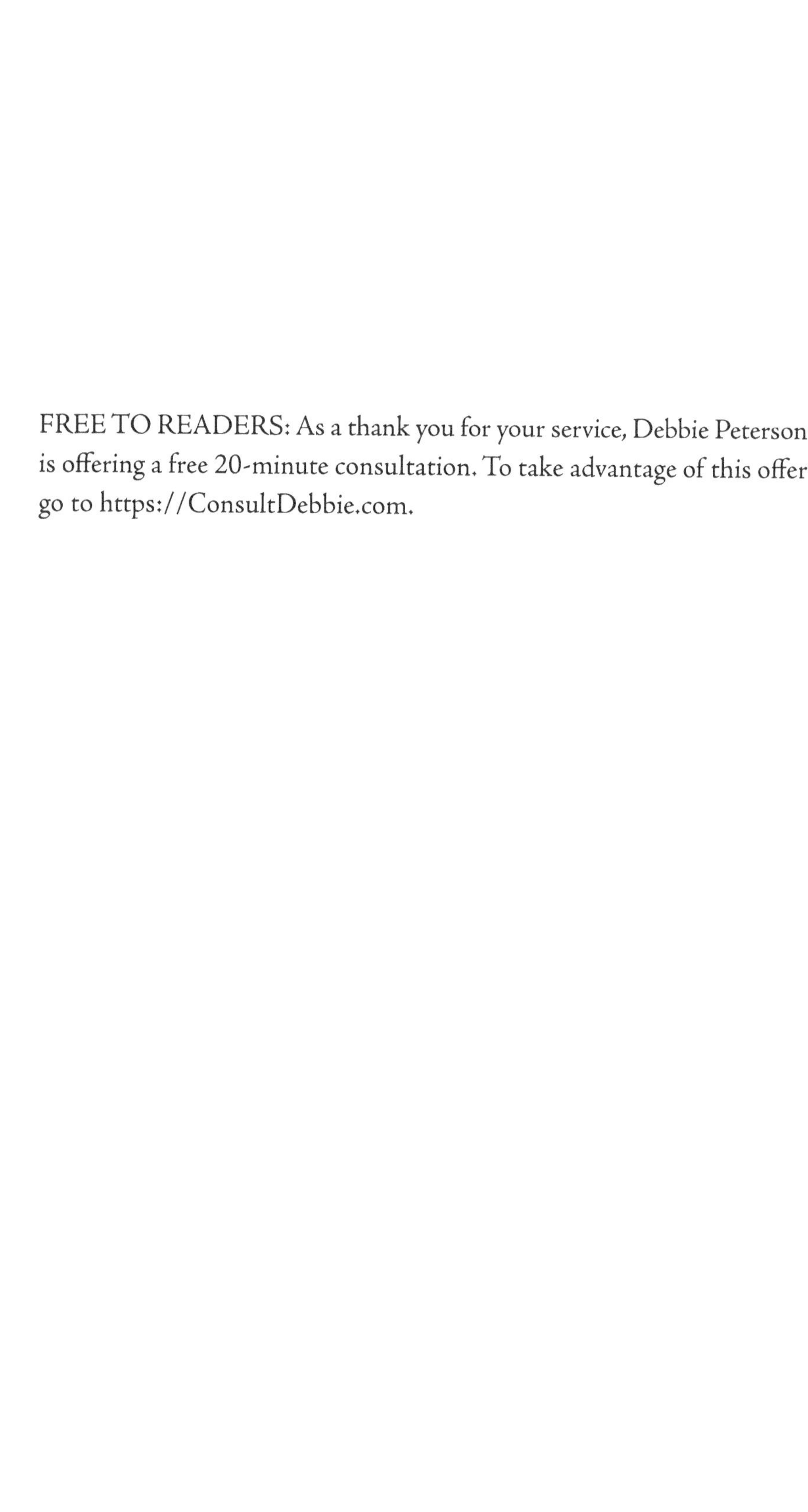

FREE TO READERS: As a thank you for your service, Debbie Peterson is offering a free 20-minute consultation. To take advantage of this offer go to https://ConsultDebbie.com.

CONTENTS

AUTHOR'S NOTE

The facts described in my book are based on my own experience in public service and advocacy, my research in government and media sources, and the experiences that were related to me by others.

Use of male pronouns does not imply gender preference.

The opinions on matters of public interest and concern are my own.

Debbie Peterson.com
Info@DebbiePeterson.com

Wherever the people have found a leader who was loyal to them; brave; and not too far ahead, there they have followed him, and there has begun the solution of our common problem; the problem of the cities, states, and nations—the problem of civilized living in human communities. —Lincoln Steffens

INTRODUCTION

Local government can be fascinatingly intriguing, significant, and captivating. This book grew out of years of determination while I was a Mayor, Councilmember, and Planning Commissioner to make local government and public meetings approachable, friendly, customer-oriented, accessible, accountable, and understood. It is a process that needs work on all sides of the dais—by the public, by staff, and by elected representatives.

As the first directly elected female Mayor of my town, I achieved all of the goals I set for my two years in office except one: I wanted to set up a course for new Councilmembers to teach them their roles and responsibilities as directors on the many Boards on which they sit. This book is my fulfillment of that goal. Boardsmanship is an art, a science, and a learned skill that isn't taught, but which would enhance the service we provide to those who elect us if we understood how to do it well. If I can serve your organization, conference, or seminar by consulting or speaking on best practices in local government, I would be delighted to do so. Please go to my speaking and workshop page at DebbiePeterson.com for more information.

I became familiar with local government practice and process by osmosis over the course of thirteen years. You can do that too, but you will be much more effective and waste much less time if you learn how it works before you take up your role. This book gives you the background, the job description, and the playbook to hit the ground running.

In local government, as in any communication, there are sending and receiving sides. In this case, The People of a community are the senders, and you, as their elected representative, are the receiver. Representatives must know what the represented want.

The more informed you are, and the more the senders communicate with you, the better the quality of life for all of you.

The problem is that there is no playbook, no job description, no education for newly elected representatives or for the public that explains what is expected of us and what our jobs are. It's all happenstance. The electeds get thrown in at the deep end, and their constituents often don't even get to the pool, or they check in with their representatives in a haphazard way.

It took me six years in public service to understand all of this. The California League of Cities, of which many Cities are members, holds conferences twice a year and offers good training, but attendance is voluntary, and it is hit and miss, as not all Cities are members, and not all Councilmembers attend, and if they do attend, not all Councilmembers attend government training.

I share, as an insider, a former Mayor and good government advocate, what nobody tells us going in—your roles and responsibilities. Both are critical if we are serious about governing well.

The relationship between the govern-ers and the governed is often perceived as adversarial or actually is adversarial. Neither the public nor their representatives understand how City Hall works. As a result, mistrust develops at best, and apathy at worst. Government staff and electeds may not think in terms of how to engage the public, or they may want to avoid embarrassment and get on with their work, viewing the public as a nuisance, and finding ways to do things without involving the public.

But it didn't start out this way, and it isn't intended in our national or State Constitutions to be this way. We The People created our form of government to serve us. The very first amendment in our federal and in most State Constitutions, is FREEDOM OF SPEECH. The governed are to speak their truth. We are to be a government by committee. The institutions of our government belong to those who are governed. They are in charge. Your job is to serve them.

I will suggest exercises that will enhance your knowledge: something interesting or entertaining to think about, google, complete, or watch.

I will provide you with:

- How-tos

- Practical actions that get results

- Helpful exercises

- Real life examples

- Occasional comic relief

- Worksheets—Food for thought

- A template for public records requests

Before we get started you should know a little bit about me:

- I was the Mayor of the small town of Grover Beach, California for two years. From 2004 through 2019 I served as an appointed Planning Commissioner, elected Councilmember, and Mayor. As a directly elected Mayor, I now carry the lifetime title of "The Honorable."

- I have written four books, the most recent of which chronicles my time in office.

- I have a Communications degree in Public Relations.

- I have worked alongside hundreds of people who want to improve their communities.

- I was named the Young Business Personality of Scotland.

- I worked for development agencies as a consultant to startup companies and companies repurposing in restructuring, marketing, product development, manufacturing, and food production.

- I was taught Boardsmanship by the chairman of an international bank.

- I set up my first Board at the age of twenty-four.

Here's what this book is and what it isn't:

- It is based on my personal experience as an active participant in local government.

- The stories and examples are real situations that occurred while I was in office.

- Public discourse can be disconcerting, and the truth can be ugly. My objective is to provide Positive, Constructive, Win-Win outcomes.

- It is not intended to be party political. In fact, it is the opposite—it is nonpartisan.

- 'Nonpartisan' means that solutions are based on the premise that we all have a part in problem-solving on a local level that transcends the limitations of political maneuvering.

- It is the story of everyday people who serve their communities and have the power to set up good government.

The most effective local governance happens when Councilmembers, Citizens, and City Hall participate together to improve our communities. Local government affects our day-to-day lives more than any other branch of the government, and yet, I never learned anything about it in school, and as far as I can tell, it is not taught now, either. It is the one level of government that we are most able to impact, that in turn will influence government up the line to County, State, and federal levels. In *City Council 101* you will discover how to change our political present and future, and you will be equipped to do so.

I have organized the book in the order I think is most helpful in coming to grips with what it means at a local level to be a government of The People. You do not have to read the book in order or from cover to cover. We all come to the dais with unique experience, knowledge, skills, and abilities. You may already know or understand some of the information. You may find that what you thought you knew doesn't work in a government context, so come with an open mind. You can skip back and forth between the topics.

Communication has been my life's work, whether it's marketing my business, or being forever changed by experiencing a new culture, or somehow finalizing a real estate transaction when it seemed the parties would never find a way through, or writing a book, or as a public servant seeing that often people are totally in the dark about the work of their government, whether by default or by design. For those who begin their service completely uninitiated in politics or government law, as I did, herein is how it works, when it doesn't work, and how it could work.

REFERENCES

- *United States Constitution, State Constitutions*—Free Speech

- *The Brown, or 'Sunshine' Act* (California)—Open Meetings

- *Fair Political Practices Act* (U.S.A.)—Finance, Campaign Disclosure

- *Robert's Rules of Order*—Meetings

You have probably observed by now that I capitalize words that many do not. These are the words that matter in good governance—The People and their institutions.

PART I

WHO DO YOU WORK FOR?

In corresponding with his wife, Abigail, a month after the *Declaration of Independence* was approved by the thirteen colonies, John Adams asserted that in public office the country needs "Statesmen, Heroes, and Philosophers." Reflect on your pledge of allegiance and your oath of office in the weeks and months ahead. Which will you be?

CHAPTER 1 SO, YOU GOT ELECTED. NOW WHAT?

This chapter focuses on the roles and responsibilities of local elected representatives. We will explore the job description of these elected officials and how it differs from the other job descriptions and Boards you may have come across. I will provide real life examples of my experiences as a Councilmember and Mayor.

Vocabulary:

Half Staff vs Half Mast	
Chair/President/Mayor	Interchangeable: the person leading a meeting
Mayor Pro Tem/Vice Mayor	Are the same
Police Powers	

Voters elect candidates based on their campaign platform and promises and on the citizens' expectations of their elected representatives. The People are the boss of the representatives they elect.

When I was first elected Mayor, as soon as the count was certified, I found myself overwhelmed by the thought, "I don't know how to be a Mayor! What do I do now; what do I do next?" I knew what I wanted to achieve, I was clear in my goals and well informed, and I had diligently researched the new committees of which I would be a member. However, I had no idea of the more intangible side—like, how to BE a Mayor.

About a week into my term, I went to lunch at a local Italian restaurant. The personable owner congratulated me and with rare insight, asked if I had seen the film, *The Candidate*, starring Robert Redford. Redford plays a Senate candidate who gets elected and finds himself completely at a loss when he wins. He plays it exactly as I had felt it, saying, "What am I supposed to do now?" We had a good laugh because it was so true.

For example, one of the things I didn't know as the Mayor-elect was that the City Manager would call on me if there was a suggestion that the flag should be at **half-staff** to honor a fallen hero. No one else gets to decide whether the City flag goes to half-staff; not even the President. It is the Mayor who makes that call. I didn't even know that half-staff is the correct term, not half-mast. Half-mast is for boats. Staff is for flag poles. When there was a shooting I wondered, should I go and be with the citizens, or should I let the first responders get on with their jobs.

I was fortunate to have a friend who was not only a first responder, but who had for 15 years been a faithful observer of local government. He had seen how the best representatives worked, and how those not so good, did also. He kept me right on a number of things. When the shooting occurred, he said, "Debbie, people want the Mayor to be there. They need you there." Not necessarily while it was happening, but soon after.

When a public figure died, he alerted me that the City Manager would soon be calling to ask if I wanted the City flags at half-staff.

On election night I experienced what is NOT a Councilmember's job. The Dixieland band had just quit playing, we had consumed the sugar cookies with red, white, and blue icing. It was 8 pm, time for the first vote count to show up at the County. As we gathered around the TV monitor squinting at the tiny figures rolling down the screen, trying to confirm that I had actually won the election, the Vice-Mayor for the Mayor I would be succeeding, sidled up to me and whispered in my ear, "So, Debbie, what do you want me to do?"

Not only was his timing inept, but I was stunned that he would make such a request. However, it was not out of character based on the way he approached his role as the Vice Mayor of our town. He was old-school military and viewed his role as the right hand of the Mayor, with the Mayor as the top brass and himself as the next in command. If the Mayor said, 'jump' he would jump. He took his marching orders from the Mayor, acting as he was told, voting as he was told.

In my town the Mayor appoints his **Vice Mayor**, who is sometimes also referred to as the '**Mayor Pro Tem**,' a Latin term meaning 'for the time being.' I certainly hadn't appointed him as MY Vice Mayor, so perhaps he also viewed his role as a Councilmember in the same manner—he took orders from the Mayor. But the Council is not a military institution. We are not at war. We do not need the same strict adherence to a leader's command. We are independently elected individuals who determine the direction of the City. We are the local Legislative branch, or estate, of government that makes the laws.

Councilmembers, even Mayors Pro Tem, are not like the cartoon character 'Deputy Dog' who is a constant, 'yes sir, yes sir' to the sheriff, saluting and carrying out orders. If there is any 'yes sir, yes sir' it should be to the Citizens of our communities.

I gave him my first and last order: he should do as he thought best, should vote as his conscience guided, and that I would not, as Mayor, be giving him orders. He was to make up his own mind as an independent member of the Council with his one vote of five. In most Cities the Mayor is the ceremonial head and chairs the Council meetings. The Mayor is not the Chief Executive. That is the job of the City Manager hired by Council majority vote. The Mayor is just one vote of five votes on the Council. As Councilmembers, even as Mayors, we give direction not as individuals but only through the majority vote of the Council. These decisions are then carried out by the City Manager who is hired by the Council. The Council also hires the City Attorney who advises on legal matters. Councilmembers do not take part in the day-to-day decisions or management of the City.

Addressing current issues is a critical role of Board and

Councilmembers. It is the Board's responsibility to face real problems and solve them with real answers. We are tasked with this responsibility when we are elected. The public expects this of us.

The system falls down because at the City level we are volunteers, many of whom work 40 or more hours a week in addition to our public and personal responsibilities. In my County, there is little formal training to help newly elected representatives.

We come from a variety of backgrounds with a variety of skill sets, experience, and intellect. As a result, oversight can lapse due to an absence of knowledge of the roles and responsibilities of the position. The "common man" makeup of the City Council means the necessary financial, legal, or human relations knowledge to ask the right questions to make sure The People's business is being well managed may not exist on the Council.

NOTES

 # THE JOB DESCRIPTION

Vocabulary:

Jurisdiction	The area a government agency or representative serves.
Recall Election	A special election called to remove and replace a sitting official.
Oath of Office	Required of all elected and "sworn" officials.

So, what are the marching orders? What is the job of a Councilmember or Mayor or the Vice Mayor?

Qualifications: The Voters of a City determine its election rules. Candidates must usually have at least 6 months residency in the City and be at least eighteen years of age.

Tenure: Usually two- to four-year terms.

Pay: Sometimes extraordinarily little. When I started as a Councilmember in 2008 it was $300 a month—not enough even to cover car expenses, and no benefits. Most Councils are a little more generous and pay more now. Some larger Cities pay in the hundreds of thousands.

Termination: once elected, apart from death, only five events can remove an elected representative before the term is up:

- **Conviction of a Felony** If charged, the process often takes longer than a two- or four-year term of office.

- **Resignation**

- **A medical condition** so serious that the Councilmember misses four consecutive months of meetings, in which case the Council may appoint a replacement.

- **Moving out of the jurisdiction** of the agency.

A successful recall election, which is time consuming and expensive, and, in the end, voters decide if the Councilmember should or should not be recalled.

State Constitutions set out the roles of Cities. I am in California, so I will use my own State, County, and City terminology and structure as examples. Although the terminology may change from locale to locale, the principles are the same. If a City is a **Charter City**, it does not run its City by the boilerplate State Constitution rules that bind the rest of the **General Law** Cities. It has its own Constitution, or "charter." Most Cities, however, are not Charter Cities and therefore must follow the constructs set out by the State Constitution for general law Cities.

According to the California Constitution Councilmembers must do three things:

1. They must attend Council meetings

2. They arrange for the appointment of a Chief of Police

3. They swear an oath of allegiance to the federal and their State Constitutions

As a rule, Councilmembers take part in City events, but they don't have to do so. Councilmembers represent their City on local Boards, usually regional or Cunty Boards that meet twice monthly, monthly, or every other month. Conscientious Councilmembers read and research staff reports before the weekly, or twice monthly Council meetings and committee meetings, attend meetings, respond when community members reach out to them, and report back to the Council on the activities of the committees on which they serve.

In most California Cities, the Mayor is the spokesperson for the City.

The following is the **sworn statement** required by the California Constitution and administered by the City Clerk:

> "I will support and defend the Constitution of the United States and the Constitution of the State of California against all enemies, foreign and domestic; I will bear true faith and allegiance to the Constitution of the United States and the Constitution of the State of California; I take this obligation freely, without any mental reservation or purpose of evasion; I will well and faithfully discharge the duties upon which I am about to enter."

Does this statement of allegiance constitute subordination to the will of the Mayor by the Vice Mayor, such as I described of the Vice Mayor in Chapter One? Here's what ten former U.S. Defense Secretaries appointed by their respective Presidents said in a joint opinion article in the *Washington Post* on January 3, 2020:

> *"Each of us swore an oath to support and defend the Constitution against all enemies, foreign and domestic. We did not swear it to an individual or a party."*
>
> –Ashton Carter, Dick Cheney, William Cohen, Mark Esper, Robert Gates, Chuck Hagel, James Mattis, Leon Panetta, William Perry, and Donald Rumsfeld

Q. Who Is Your Boss?

A. Is it:_____

    a. The President ?

    b. The City Manager ?

    c. The District Attorney ?

    d. We, The People ?

If you chose a. The President, you were somewhat correct. The President runs the Executive branch of the Federal Government that is tasked with carrying out the country's laws. Federal laws supersede local laws in most cases. However, Cities are independent units of governance and as such City Councilmembers are not employed by the President.

If you chose b. The City Manager, you got it completely backwards. The City Manager is employed by majority vote of the City Council. The Council directs the manager, not vice versa. The City Manager's role is that of the chief of the executive function of the City, responsible for carrying out the laws, and the Council and its members are subject to those laws.

If you chose c. The District Attorney (DA), you understand that if you violate open meeting or open government laws the DA is the first line of enforcement of The People's right to oversee their public institutions. However, the DA is not the Council's boss.

You will know by now that elected representatives and public officials work for The People. Collectively we have created and own our government institutions and are the ultimate employers of those we elect and those who run the institutions. The buck stops with The People. It is our money that runs the institution, and it is our lives, livelihoods, personal safety, and quality of life that the institutions protect. The correct answer is d. We, The People.

Before You Get Started: Attend as many City Council and committee meetings as you can and view others online so that you are up to date on current events and the history of the community. You can also read agenda packets to get up to date.

Once elected: Go to Council meetings of others with whom you will serve on local committees and during public comment congratulate them on their election.

Make your message count: Watch a meeting online and review the presentation of speakers from the public and/or on the dais, so you can learn from them what works and doesn't work in this particular venue and so you are more at ease from the outset.

Entertainment

Watch *The Candidate* starring Robert Redford available from $1.99 at Google Play Movies & TV, Apple TV, Amazon Prime Video, and YouTube.

NOTES

____

____

____

____

____

____

____

____

____

 # LOCAL GOVERNMENT 101

Vocabulary

General Law vs. Charter Cities	
Police Powers	
Elected vs. Appointed Mayor	
Council-Manager vs. Strong Mayor	
Planning Commission	
Board of Supervisors/City Council/ Special District/Joint Powers Authority/Committee	

Local government in the United States has evolved uniquely from State to State, County to County, even City to City. Local government has always existed, whether voted upon, chosen by a king or the church, elected by a group of fellow worthies, or imposed by a conqueror. As I did, you may sense that local government is different from State or federal government and as I did, you may struggle to fully grasp how or why.

The organization of local politics is confusing because it **is** set up differently from State or federal systems, and the lines of representation are drawn differently. The US Constitution did not address local government, although State Constitutions do make provision for Cities. Cities and Counties expanded in response to population increases. Cities were an experiment akin to the wild west where the City evolved faster than the law, like an entrepreneurial business start-up that takes off and catches up as it evolves.

Local government is usually set up to be non-partisan, based on the ideal that solving local problems is not party political.

In California, the powers of the Cities are found in Article 11, section 7, of the State Constitution that describes the power of all Cities, and section 5 that describes the power of Charter Cities. Most cities in California are general law Cities; however, Cities that pre-date the State Constitution may use the charter adopted prior to Statehood. Charter Cities can override general State laws.

Cities are unique because they are independent. Although they are governed by the State Constitution, Cities are not subdivisions of the State as Counties are.

A County is a political subdivision of the state, organized to carry out some functions of state government in unincorporated areas of a State, whereas a City is an incorporation of the inhabitants of a specified region for purposes of local government.

California Government Code section 36505 allows a County or City to make and enforce within its limits all local police, sanitary and other ordinances and regulations not in conflict with general laws. The police power granted by the Constitution is "the power of local governments to legislate for the general welfare."

I'd like to pause here to explain police power further so that it is not confused with the power of individual police officers or police departments.

Police powers are the ability of a government to enact laws to regulate its citizenry. The term does not relate to the common connotation of police as officers charged with maintaining public order, but to broad governmental regulatory power. Berman v. Parker, a 1954 U.S. Supreme Court case, stated that "public safety, public health, morality, peace and quiet, law and order... are some of the more conspicuous examples of the traditional application of the police power."

The division of police power in the United States is delineated in the Tenth Amendment, which states that "the powers not delegated to the United States by the Constitution, nor prohibited by it to the states, are reserved to the states respectively, or to the people." That is, in the United States, the federal government does not hold a general police power but may only act where the Constitution enumerates a power. It is the States, then, that hold the general police power. This is a central tenet to the system of federalism, which the U.S. Constitution embodies.

A State's regulatory power, therefore, is incredibly broad.

As Cities have evolved, so has the definition of "public welfare" until now it embraces regulations "to promote the economic welfare, convenience, and general prosperity of the community."

For example, General Law Cities can decide whether they will adopt a City Manager form of government, or whether the Mayor will be the Chief Executive, and whether they will have an **elected, rather** than **Council-appointed** Mayor. (Gov. Code §§ 34800 and 34900.) The Council elects one of its members as Mayor on an annual basis unless a municipal ordinance approved by the electorate provides for election by popular vote. In recognition of the importance of local elected government, a **Directly Elected Mayor**, unlike County Supervisors, carries a special place as the head of a City, even if only ceremonial, and the lifetime title of "The Honorable."

In General Law Cities the City Council consists of five Councilmembers, including the Mayor, each with an equal vote. Acting as a body, it is the chief governing authority. In Charter Cities the size of the Council may be greater.

The **Council-manager** system has become the most popular in California. It was developed in an effort to avoid the corruption and inefficiency of political machines in Cities in the late 1800s. It envisions a professional, nonpolitical public administrator who is responsible to the Council for enforcement of City ordinances, direction of administrative operations, and technical advice. The Manager is appointed by and serves at the pleasure of the Council. The Council retains sole authority to enact local laws, make policy decisions, approve programs, adopt the budget, and provide general direction to the Manager but does not manage on a day-to-day basis.

Charter Cities may employ the **strong Mayor system** in which the

Mayor is the executive head of all departments in addition to presiding over Council meetings. However, no system will function effectively without an informed and active citizenry.

City **Planning Commissions** are appointed by City Councils to deal with just one area of the public's business—land-use. Planning Commissions make most decisions on land-use based on existing laws. They may advise on, but they do not create those laws, and their decisions can be appealed to the City Council.

City Councilmembers and Mayors serve on regional Boards of **Special Districts** and **Joint Powers Authorities** that have wide-ranging powers to affect their communities. These agencies tax, apply for and dispense State and federal grant funds and allocations, and decide how to divest the millions of dollars raised by local, State, and federal taxes. Late-night television political commentator John Oliver, in his sometimes crass and often hilarious political commentary, *Last Week Tonight*, devoted an entire show to Special Districts. He calls Special Districts "Ghost Government" because they are seldom seen and work in the dark.[1]

In some Cities, the Mayor assigns Council representatives to these Boards. In other Cities, as in mine, appointments are made by consensus unless State government code, or Mayoral meddling make it otherwise.

Special Districts are established by Counties, with budgets approved by the County Board of Supervisors, and accountability to the State. Special Districts (SDs) are enterprise organizations set up to run as small businesses to manage specific services such as fire, sewer, and water for multiple communities or **unincorporated** areas of a **County**. Another agency hybrid, **Joint Powers Authorities** run special projects or activities, often public-private projects. These agency Boards are not directly elected, but are made up of Councilmembers, Mayors, and County Supervisors. Some Special Districts, such as the Air Pollution Control Districts are set up by the State, giving the Chief Executive sole power with no appeal to his decision except to an appeal committee

---

1 March 6, 2016, *Last Week Tonight* show (https://www.youtube.com/watch?v=3saU5racsGE)

that he appoints. He can only be curbed if the Board fires him.

In the hierarchy of government agencies, Counties, managed by an elected Board of Supervisors, have wide latitude in deciding what municipal services they need and will provide. County laws take precedence over City laws unless the City wishes to make stricter laws. State law and our State Constitutions eclipse County and City laws, and federal laws and our U.S. Constitution supersede all States, Counties, Cities, and Special Districts. Each City, County, State, and the federal government has its own laws with different areas of legal and geographical authority that sometimes overlap.(Cal.Const. § 1 (a).) The County exercises only the powers of the State, granted by the State, and was created for the purpose of advancing the policy of the State at large.

"What does a [County] Supervisor supervise? A County Supervisor supervises the County government. The Board of Supervisors doesn't supervise the Citizens. The Citizens elect this person to do their work to keep the County government in line—IN LINE. Not the other way around. So, when you see People like the County manager or the public health director dictating policy past the Board it should not be that way. The Board of Supervisors supervises them." –Steve Schumann

PART 2

The Dais, the Podium, and the Lectern

"You gotta serve somebody. It may be the devil; it may be the Lord, but you gotta serve somebody." –Bob Dylan

The Dais, pronounced 'Day Us' or 'Die Us' is a **Podium**—the raised platform on which the Council sits—Latin for "foot."

The **Lectern** is the 'standing desk' from which a speaker delivers a message. The error most everyone makes is to call the Lectern a Podium. It is not a **Podium**. It is a Lectern.

I learned the correct use of the term 'Podium' when I was a member of Toastmasters. I highly recommend joining a Toastmasters group even for a year, if you wish to speak in public. It is a friendly opportunity to gain experience in the skills of public speaking. I remember how terrified I was when I took my required speechmaking class in college. It was the best thing that could have happened to me. It taught me to be comfortable speaking in public.

Exercise: Attend a Local Toastmasters Meeting to see if it's something that would be useful to you.

NOTES

____

____

____

____

____

____

____

____

____

____

 # HOW DO YOU GET THINGS DONE AROUND HERE?

Vocabulary

Chair/President/Mayor	Used interchangeably for the person leading a meeting
Estates	
Constitution/Charter/Bylaws	Rules by which an organization is run and to which the Board must adhere
Council/Board/Committee	Ruling body of an organization
Be the dog and not the tail	
Findings, Ordinances, and Resolutions	Aspects of Legislation

My first question when I was elected as a City Councilmember was "How do you get things done around here?" First, I asked a former Mayor. He looked unsure and quickly changed the subject. So I asked the City Manager. He, too, seemed baffled by the question and introduced me to the City department heads. I asked each of them, and I got the same unsettled response. I was asking while wearing my management consulting hat. If I put on my Councilmember hat I can explain that on a Council of five members I need two other votes to get anything done because three votes out of five is a majority. Since I can only talk to one Councilmember outside of a public meeting (otherwise I have discussed Council business with a majority of the Council outside of the public view) I will have to convince at least one other Councilmember to vote my way at the next meeting. But it's not as easy as that because we cannot vote until any issue has been completely researched and aired before the public.

Going back to my question of the former Mayor and City Staff, I determined that if something were important to me, I would ask nicely as often as was needed until I got what I wanted or at least until it was agendized. That usually works. Impassioned pleas also work if they aren't over-used.

If there are potentially tens of thousands of voters participating, how do we get ANYTHING done around here? We are a Constitutional Republic with a democratic system, i.e., we elect you as the legislative Board to oversee our governance and you appoint the executive department to take care of the day-to-day decisions rather than a Democracy in which we The People vote on each one ourselves.

Be the Dog; Not the Tail

But however new you are to the job, it is your responsibility on the Board to be the dog and not the tail. It's easy for new Councilmembers to begin to think of themselves either as City Employees, or to rely on the City Manager to tell them how to do their jobs. This can lead to delegating your authority as an elected representative of The People in your jurisdiction to the City Manager and his staff. That is not the role of a Board member, and it can be dangerous to get too cozy with the City Manager and the City Attorney, even sometimes with fellow Councilmembers because as a Board member you are to think independently and act in the best interests of the voters. In other words, you are the dog and not the tail. The tail should not be wagging you; you should be wagging the tail. It is your job to oversee the City Manager and set the vision for your community. Sometimes a City Attorney or staff member will go beyond providing staff reports and answering questions, to attempting to participate in Board deliberation.

This is the job of the dog, not the tail, and the tail should remain quiet unless asked to speak by a Councilmember. The City Manager is there to manage the City under the Board's direction, not to manage the Board.

NOTES

 # SUNLIGHT IS GOOD FOR EVERYONE

VOCABULARY

Robert's Rules of Order	
The Brown Act	
The First Amendment	

Robert's Rules of Order is the rule book for how to conduct a meeting. The **Brown Act** is the open meeting rule book for local elected officials in California. However, the principles of open government and freedom of speech are the same at all levels of government and from State to State. Pulling from the Brown Act, they are:

- The People do not yield our sovereignty to the agencies that serve us.

- The People delegate authority, but do not give our public servants the right to decide what is good for us to know and what is not good for us to know.

- The People insist on remaining informed so we can retain control over the institutions we have created.

- Public servants must comply with the open government legislation:

- ▫ Completely
- ▫ Faithfully
- ▫ Uninterruptedly

- ♦ No act or budget constraint can:
  - ▫ Suspend
  - ▫ Eliminate
  - ▫ Otherwise modify the legal obligation and duty of agencies to fully comply

The foundational principals are that the public Commissions, Boards, and Councils and the other public agencies exist to aid in the conduct of The People's business. Their actions must be taken openly, and their deliberations must be conducted openly. For all the reasons discussed in this course, it is critical to have trained Council and staff members and an attorney present at meetings to ensure that the law is enforced in a manner that protects and honors the rights of the public to whom the institution belongs.

Take the time to review and refer back to open government legislation over and over. You will find that it comes to life as you begin to monitor your own government agencies and yourself.

The Sunshine [Brown] Act (California)

Complete, faithful, and uninterrupted compliance with the Sunshine Act is a matter of overriding public importance. No future enactments shall suspend, eliminate, or modify the legal obligation and duty of local agencies to fully comply in a complete, faithful, and uninterrupted manner.[2]

The biggest surprise to me when I was first appointed as a Planning Commissioner was the rules of engagement for Board decision-making.

---

2 The Ralph M Brown Act 54954.4. (c) Ralph M. Brown Act [Chapter 9 (commencing with Section 54950) of Part 1 of Division 2 of Title 5 of the Government Code] Chapter 641 of the Statutes of 1986.

In business, decisions about Board agenda items are decided on the golf course or other venue with other Board members long before the vote in the meeting. While I didn't golf, as a company director and chair of my manufacturing company, I met with or lunched with fellow Board members one-by-one to provide them with the background on issues on the agenda, to gain their input, listen to their advice, present my case, and thrash out solutions well before we met as a Board. Board action was nothing more than summarizing concurring views, rubber-stamping decisions, and making sure they were minuted. Pre-meeting Board decision-making is good practice in all organizations except government or quasi-government organizations, such as homeowner associations.

What you must know even before being elected is that as a Councilmember, it is considered a secret meeting if you discuss your position on any item on the agenda with a majority of the Councilmembers anywhere or any time apart from in public on the dais. That does not, however, stop you from talking with a minority of Council colleagues, as long as you do not converse with a Council majority outside an agendized public meeting. The running of government is the business of The People and is to be open to The People and run by the wishes of the majority of The People. It is a much longer process than making business decisions because it is decision-making by committee.

The Brown Act elucidates the role of government agencies as the instruments of The People's business. It clarifies the role of The People as the institution owners who do not yield their sovereignty to the agencies that serve them. It decrees that although The People delegate authority to their public servants, **they do not give their public servants the right to decide what they should and should not know** [emphasis mine]. It insists that only by being informed are The People able to retain control over the institutions of their creation. The Act **allows for greater openness than its minimum standards** and demands that **government agencies comply completely and in good faith**. It mandates that nothing can take away these rights. The Brown Act governs local agencies in California.

Across the country at the local, State, and national level, similar legislation protects the business of The People.

When I was on the Planning Commission, I learned the basics of the Brown Act. The Planning Commission was gracious in its discussion of contentious aspects of projects. We treated one another and the public respectfully, often calling project representatives back to the lectern to provide further information.

NOTES

____

____

____

____

____

____

____

____

____

____

The City of Grover Beach encourages all residents and interested parties to participate in City government meetings. Your participation and presence are essential to good government.

The following items are posted in PDF format. Your computer must have Adobe Acrobat Reader, which allows you to view, navigate, and print files in this format across all major computing platforms for free.

Date / Time: Monday, November 4, 2019 at 6:00 p.m.
Location: Council Chamber, 154 S. 8th Street, Grover Beach, CA
Regular Meeting—Agenda Regular Meeting—Agenda Packet

Item 1. Proclamation for National Hospice Palliative Care Month

Presentation None

Consent—City Council
Item 2. Draft Minutes of City Council Meeting, Monday, October 21, 2019
Item 3. Professional Services Agreement for a Senior Center Feasibility Study
Item 4. Resolution to Submit an Application for the SB 3 Planning Grants Program
Item 5. Award of Construction Contract Measure K-14 Street Improvements CIP 2295-9
Item 6. Community Development Block Grant (CDBG) Water Main Project (CIP 4267—2020): Award of Professional Design Engineering Services

Public Hearing
Item 7. Introduction and First Reading of an Ordinance to Amend Municipal Code Article VIII Building Regulations Chapter 1 to Adopt by Reference the 2019 California Building Codes and 2018 International Property Maintenance Code with Local Amendments

Regular Business
Item 8. Economic Development Activities
Item 9. Monterey Bay Community Power Policy Board Memorandum of Understanding
Amended Attachment No. 1

Please note: Staff reports may be large files that take time to download, depending upon your Internet connection speed. Contact the City Clerk's Office at (805) 473-4567 if you have any problems accessing a file.

Any supplemental items received after copying / distribution of the agenda packet are available at Grover Beach City Hall, 154 South Eighth Street.

A printed public counter copy of the complete agenda packet is available during regular business hours at the customer service counter at Grover Beach City Hall, 154 South Eighth Street.

Most government agencies post Board meetings, notices agendas, agenda packets, and minutes online. The agenda below the chapter heading is the agenda available on my **City's website**. It includes links to each item on the agenda, including a PDF copy of each item and provides further helpful information about the agenda. It is user-friendly and welcoming.

Conscientious Councilmembers and the informed public read the staff report and do their own research. This is a challenge when agendas are not posted until 72 hours prior to a meeting. The short lead time is not entirely unreasonable because staff often must provide lengthy reports on complex issues and may need considerable time to gather current information and prepare reports for the agenda packet.

A good staff **report** explains how neighboring communities tackle the issue, informs on community impacts, pros, and cons, includes easy to understand budget and cost information, and implications of alternative solutions. Staff often make a recommendation and provide the motion for adoption and should also provide alternatives to the recommended course of action. If not, the report is incomplete. So, while Sunshine laws allow for posting agendas earlier than the minimum 72 hours prior to a meeting, it will not usually be possible.

Once the chairperson or Mayor **Open**s the meeting, it is followed by a **Moment Of Silence**, the **Flag Salute,** and the **Roll Call** so that a quorum can be confirmed (in the case of five Councilmembers three must be present in order for the Council to vote on agenda items.)

This Council holds **closed sessions** at the end of meetings, so most members do not wait around for the session to end in order to hear the legally required **Report Of Action Taken** following the closed session. Taking an additional opportunity to report the action at the next Council meeting so that the public are aware of it, as shown in this agenda, is a good practice.

Next is anything of a **Ceremonial** nature—community proclamations, or City awards to Citizens. Usually there is a time in the agenda for the public communications not related to agenda items. Often it is at the beginning of the meeting. Public comment on agenda items is opened when the agenda items are heard.

While not legally required, except for public hearings, ideally, every item on the agenda will be open to public comment, and the agenda will publish the rules of order so members of the public know how to participate. Transparency is the order of the day. Confidentiality is limited to confidential employee matters and negotiations. Speech is limited only in that it must conform to orderly safe conduct, relevancy to the agenda item, or if in general public comment, is under the purview of the Council or Board.

Public Communications provide an opportunity for members of the public to address the Council on matters not on the agenda. In most cases the chair legitimately limits how long each member of the public may comment, depending on the size of the crowd, to keep the meeting moving. This is not a question-and-answer session. It is a violation of the Brown Act to discuss matters raised during public communications because they have not been agendized. Comments are to be addressed to the chair; not to individual Councilmembers, and the chair determines whether or not any action will occur on the comments.

While it is important to stick with the order of items on the agenda out of respect for those attending, there are times when it is better to change the order. With a large audience it helps to determine how many members of the audience are present for a particular item and to move the item nearer to the front of the agenda. If the agenda matter concerns families or children in the audience it may be better to move the matter to an earlier time in the meeting. The chair's role is to facilitate the smooth running of the meeting.

A good chairperson will poll the crowd during the **Agenda Review** and ask the Council to approve rearranging the agenda to ensure public hearings that have the most members of the public present are heard early in the meeting. While frustrating to members of the public, the usual 2–3-minute limit on each public comment is good meeting hygiene. Otherwise, Councilmembers get punchy after hours on the dais, their decision-making capacity is compromised, and members of the public go home, weary of sitting and waiting for their agenda item to come up. If the chair does not have good meeting control and a clear understanding of the point of the meeting, the business of the Council cannot be completed efficiently and effectively. The best public process will take place at the meeting itself if the chair of the meeting explains how the meeting will be run and gives reminder updates as it goes along, so members of the public can follow along and know how and when to participate.

Consent agenda items are those that are usual and customary matters that don't necessitate a hearing but do need Council approval. They are usually agreed as a group. Individual items can be pulled from the agenda if Councilmembers have questions or if members of the public wish to comment.

Next on the agenda is a **Public Hearing**. Public Hearings are for **Ordinance**s and **Resolution**s that will require at least two hearings. **Regular Business** items are those which are more of an informational nature that do not require two hearings but that need to be approved by the Council and require neither a Resolution nor an Ordinance.

For items that require a public hearing and regular business, or even consent agenda items that are "pulled" for discussion by the Council, there is a prescribed procedure that protects public participation and ensures that decisions are made in the open following public input.

First, the item is announced by the chair. Then there is usually a staff report followed by questions from the Council. Following that the public make comments and finally, the Council deliberates, a motion is made, and a vote taken. The proposed resolution or ordinance should be attached to the staff report. New ordinances must have at least two public hearings before being finalized.

Sometimes Councilmembers lose track of or don't understand the process and assert their views during the pre-deliberative question time. If Councilmembers do so, they are obstructing the democratic process because they have failed to hear from the public or deliberate with the Council before reaching conclusions. If this happens, a good chairperson will redirect the

Councilmember, asking them to stick to questions and hold their opinions until Council deliberations after they have heard from the public.

Understandably frustrating to members of the public is that they only get one opportunity to speak on agenda items, usually for two to three minutes per commenter, and they are not able to respond to final comments and deliberations made by the Council, including those which may be snarky, untrue, or just plain confused. You may also have had public input in the form of emails or letters included with the staff report or later if received after the agenda was published.

As the **Chair** of the Planning Commission, I usually facilitated deliberation between the commissioners and did not participate, which is best practice, but not a requirement. In one case I made a passionate plea asking fellow commissioners to deny a project when a telecommunications company wanted to put a powerful transmitter on a hilltop lot in a residential neighborhood across from a school. The lot, owned by a much more affluent neighboring City, housed a water tower and well drawing water for their use. A transmitter would provide them with lease income. A path ran alongside the lot on three sides, making it a popular shortcut to the school across the street. The tower would be sixty feet high, and while disguised as a tree, it would be the tallest "tree" in the mature ocean-view neighborhood. Even as a fake tree I would have argued that it had no place in a residential neighborhood, but something else worried me more.

There were conflicting reports as to whether the Electromagnetic Frequencies (EMFs) it emitted were harmful to children, and at what distance. I wasn't willing to put children's health on the line. The vote was 5-0 against the project. We prioritized our kids and the residential neighborhood over income for a neighboring town for which we had already provided access to our water.

EMFs have caused controversy for telecommunications companies and utilities for the past 20 years or so. There has been resistance to installation of 'Smart Meters' on people's gas, electric, and water meters. The People arguing against EMFs seemed a little "off" to me at the time, but I strongly supported their right not to be forced to have these installations and opposed additional charges if they exercised this right, even when I didn't understand their opposition.

I later learned that with a brain injury it can be difficult to find words, sometimes even to verbalize at all. It is difficult to organize thoughts, painful to converse, and there are often problems with balance or gait, many times accompanied by nerve pain or headaches. One of the problems caused by such an injury is irregular brain wave activity. I discovered that EMFs can dysregulate nerve-firing and disrupt brain wave activity for those with brain injuries. I am now even more pleased that I passionately supported the rights of children and adults to limit exposure to EMFs.

Council Committee Reports provide insight into the special committees and districts that also serve the community. These will be public meetings that you can attend if you have concerns or interest. Soon after you are elected you will likely be assigned committees on which you must represent the City. In some Cities the Mayor makes the assignments, in some it is by Council concensus, and in some cases, ordinances dictate the composition of the Board. It is a good idea to do your own research by checking the relevant ordinances, so you are sure that you are seated in accordance with the law.

In the next chapter we'll take a closer look at the agenda discussed in this chapter and other documents you will encounter in Council meetings.

Attachment 1

RESOLUTION NO. 21-

A RESOLUTION OF THE CITY COUNCIL OF THE CITY OF GROVER BEACH, CALIFORNIA, ADOPTING THE 2020 URBAN WATER MANAGEMENT PLAN AND 2020 WATER SHORTAGE CONTINGENCY PLAN AND AUTHORIZING SUBMITTAL TO THE DEPARTMENT OF WATER RESOURCES

WHEREAS, the City of Grover Beach has prepared an Urban Water Management Plan (UWMP) and Water Shortage Contingency Plan (WSCP) to satisfy the requirements of the California Water Code Sections 10610 et seq. and the Urban Water Management Planning Act of 1983; and

WHEREAS, the UWMP includes long-term resource planning tools to assure adequate water supplies are available for meeting existing and estimated future demands; and

WHEREAS, the UWMP indicates that the City has sufficient water supplies to meet current and near term demands under normal conditions and single dry year events; and

WHEREAS, the WSCP that identifies demand management and consumption reduction measures that can be adopted by the City in the event of a water supply shortage; and

WHEREAS, City staff recommends adopting the 2020 UWMP and WSCP and submitting them to the Department of Water Resources.

NOW, THEREFORE, BE IT RESOLVED by the City Council of the City of Grover Beach, California, hereby adopts the 2020 Urban Water Management Plan and Water Shortage Contingency Plan and authorized its submittal to the Department of Water Resources.

On motion by Council Member   , seconded by Council Member   , and on the following roll-call vote, to wit:

AYES:	Council Members –
NOES:	Council Members –
ABSENT:	Council Members –
ABSTAIN:	Council Members –

the foregoing Resolution was **PASSED, APPROVED,** and **ADOPTED** at a special meeting of the City Council of the City of Grover Beach, California this 13th day of December, 2021.

____
JEFF LEE, MAYOR

Attest:

____
WENDI SIMS, CITY CLERK

VOCABULARY

Defensible	Will it stand up in a court of law?
Findings	The 'Whereas' in a resolution or ordinance
Closed Session	Meetings not open to the public

Given that California is in the throes of a 1,000-year drought, this resolution sets out a good practice—keeping water conservation in the forefront.

Any ordinance or resolution must include findings. **Finding**s are the **"whereas"** clauses at the first part of an ordinance or resolution. As a rule, staff and the City Attorney draft ordinances and resolutions. The 'whereas' clauses are the legal findings in the ordinance or resolution that the Council must make to legitimately finalize any decision and to prevent legal challenges. In other words, ordinances must be '**defensible**.'

The whereas's must be true and correct, and they must conform to the proposed rule or law being enacted. The findings are usually along the lines of being in the public interest and safety and in line with Council or government policy. If directors do not find that the ordinance is supported by the information presented, then they must not vote in favor. Should these findings be unaddressed or ignored, or worse, not in accordance with the facts, the Council exposes the agency to a legal challenge, which will be costly and time-consuming; not the best use of public money and staff or Council time. The resolution here appears to be defensible.

Defensibility extends to far more than just findings on ordinances and resolutions. It includes any matter for which your Council or committee may have acted without due process or failed to operate in the open or left your agency open to lawsuits due to negligence, dereliction of duty, or failure to exercise oversight or fiscal responsibility.

Closed Session items are those few things for which the Council may meet privately—legal action, employee matters, and real estate transactions. Following the closed session the Council is required to reopen the meeting and announce any decisions made during the closed session and the votes of the individual Councilmembers on the issue, or announce that no action has been taken. The Brown Act identifies which items may be heard in closed (sometimes referred to as executive) session and even provides the appropriate headings for the agenda items. The posted agenda item must provide the names of the parties or subjects involved.

For all of the reasons discussed in this section, it is critical to have trained Council and staff members and an attorney present at meetings to ensure that the law is enforced in a manner that protects and honors the rights of the public to whom the institution belongs.

The following list of the requirements for noticing closed session items indicates how important legislators considered open meetings when they created the Brown Act:

- **License/Permit Determination**—Specify number of applicants.

- **Conference with Real Property Negotiators**—Specify street, address or parcel number, names of negotiators attending, negotiating parties, what is being negotiated, and if instruction to the negotiator involves price or payment terms.

- **Conference with Legal Counsel—Anticipated Litigation**—Significant exposure to litigation or initiation of litigation, specify how many potential cases.

- **Liability Claims**—Name of the agency the claim is against.

- **Threat to Public Services or Facilities**—Name of law enforcement agency and title of officer.

+ **Public Employment**—Description of position to be filled.

+ **Public Employee Performance Evaluation**—Specify position of employee being reviewed.

+ **Conference with Labor Negotiators**—Specify names of designated representatives, employee organization, or unrepresented employee and position of unrepresented employee.

+ **Case Review/Planning**

+ **Report Involving Trade Secret**—Specify whether discussion will concern proposed new service, program, or facility and estimated month and year of public disclosure.

+ **Hearings**—Specify whether testimony/deliberation will concern staff privileges, report of medical audit committee, or report of quality assurance committee.

+ **Conference Involving a Joint Powers Agency (JPA)**—Name of agency, all topics to be discussed using the closed session description that the JPA uses, name of local agency representative on JPA Board, names of other attendees and their agencies or representatives.

+ **Audit by California State Auditor's Office**

There are only three scenarios for which no additional information is required to be posted on the agenda:

1. **Public Employee Discipline/Dismissal/Release**—Including potential reduction of compensation.

2. **Conference with Legal Counsel—Existing Litigation**—Refer to claimant's name, names of parties, case or claim numbers unless disclosure would jeopardize service of process or existing settlement negotiations, in which case this must be specified.

3. **Charge or Complaint Involving Information Protected by Federal Law**

There is only one closed session that cannot be held in a special meeting! Why? Because special meetings can be called at irregular times and thus more easily exclude public awareness of the event.

- **Public Employee Salaries**—Description of position to be filled.

Exercise: Take a look at the following notices and see if you can identify the four Brown Act Violations committed by the Five Cities Fire authority administrator/Fire Chief, Agency Attorney, President, and Board, all of whom had served for decades. Hint: there are two violations in each of the meetings below.

August 19·2022 Five Cities Fire Authority Board Meeting.

Minutes: Five Cities Fire Authority Board Meeting   *Page 3*
Friday, August 19, 2022

BOARD COMMUNICATIONS:
Board Member Storton acknowledged the emotional response, along with support, of the Chief and FCFA staff for how they have handled the recent accident involving Engine 6692. Chair Lee thanked Engineer Bennet for participating in the Active Shooter training with Grover Beach Police Department.

CLOSED SESSION:
The Board adjourned to a Closed Session at 9:30 a.m. concerning the following item:

    b. **Public Employee Performance Evaluation, Gov. Code Section 54957**
       Position: Fire Chief/Executive Officer

RECONVENE TO OPEN SESSION:
Chair Lee called the meeting back to order at 9:46 a.m. General Counsel Hale reported after a closed session performance evaluation of Chief Lieberman that the Board has unanimously voted to put the Fire Chief at the top step of his salary range. This will result in a 3.92% increase.

ADJOURNMENT:
Chair Lee adjourned the meeting at 9:47 a.m.

SPECIAL BOARD MEETING AGENDA – SEPTEMBER 27, 2022
PAGE 2

1. **Consideration of Approval of Minutes**(MEYERS)
   Recommended Action: Approve the minutes of the Board Meeting of August 19, 2022.

2. **Consideration of Cash Disbursement Activity**(LIEBERMAN)
   Recommended Action: Receive and file the listing of cash disbursements for the period of August 1 to August 31, 2022.

3. **Consideration of Approval of an Amendment to the Fire Chief's Employment Agreement** (HALE)
   Recommended Action: Approve Amendment No. 5 to the Fire Chief/Executive Officer's employment agreement.

4. **Consideration of a Resolution Declaring Obsolete Equipment as Surplus** (LIEBERMAN)
   Recommended Action: Approve a Resolution declaring obsolete equipment as surplus.

CONTINUED BUSINESS:

None.

NEW BUSINESS:

a. **Consideration of Acceptance of Grant Award from the California Fire Foundation and Appropriate the Revenue into FY 2022-23 FCFA Budget** (LIEBERMAN)
   Recommended Action: Accept and appropriate grant funds in the amount of $13,500 from the California Fire Foundation and approve a Resolution.

BOARD MEMBER ITEMS:
The following item(s) are placed on the agenda by a Board Member who would like to receive feedback, obtain consensus to direct staff to prepare information, and/or request a formal agenda report be prepared and the item placed on a future agenda. No formal action can be taken.

None.

FIRE CHIEF ITEMS:
The following item(s) are placed on the agenda by the Fire Chief in order to receive comments, feedback and/or request direction from the Board. No formal action can be taken.

a. Fire Chief Updates

AMENDMENT NO. 5 TO
EMPLOYMENT AGREEMENT
FOR
STEPHEN C. LIEBERMAN

This Amendment No. 5 to the Employment Agreement for Stephen C. Lieberman, dated December 8, 2014, ("Agreement") is hereby made and entered into this 16th day of September, 2022 by and between the Five Cities Fire Authority, a Joint Powers Authority under California Government Code, Sections 6500 et seq., ("Authority") and Stephen C. Lieberman, an individual ("the Employee"), collectively referred to herein as ("Parties"), both of whom agree to the terms and conditions of this Amendment No. 5 to the Agreement as follows:

NOW THEREFORE, in consideration of mutual covenants herein contained, the parties agree as follows:

1.) Section 3 entitled "Salary" is modified as follows:

Authority agrees that Employee's annual base salary shall be $177,618.00 commencing on September 16, 2022. The annual base salary is payable in equal installments at the same time as other employees of Authority are paid. Subsequent increases in salary may be considered annually at the time of Employees Performance Evaluation, pursuant to Section 6 below.

2) To the extent this Amendment No. 5 is inconsistent with the Agreement dated December 8, 2014, this Amendment shall govern and prevail over the Agreement. All other provisions of the Agreement shall remain in full force and effect.

IN WITNESS WHEREOF, the Authority has caused this Amendment No. 5 to the Agreement to be signed and executed on its behalf by the Chair of the Authority Board, and duly attested by its Clerk to the Board, and Employee has signed and executed this Amendment No. 5, both in duplicate, the 16th day of September, 2022.

FIVE CITIES FIRE AUTHORITY   EMPLOYEE

_______________________________   _______________________________

Jeff Lee, Chair   Stephen C. Lieberman

1. Violation: Closed Session was agendized as Evaluation. It should also have been agendized as a salary review.

2. President reported that a salary increase had been approved. Salary increases can only be approved in open session.

SPECIAL BOARD MEETING Sept. 27th:
Agenda item 3.

1. Salary increases may only be heard in regular meetings, not special meetings.

2. The salary increase was implemented September 16th after it was illegally agreed on August 19th, before it was illegally approved on September 27th, and before the Authority could legally consider it at their next regular scheduled meeting in October, which was cancelled. The Brown Act requires that it be voided until such time as it is legally approved in a regular meeting.

Let's take a look at some of the paperwork that comes along with public meetings in the order you will usually encounter it.

The following City of Grover Beach NOTICE OF PUBLIC HEARING is excellent. The meeting is scheduled for the regular City Council date and time. It explains the many ways to participate and gives time frames for submitting comments. It even explains that other things may be included on the agenda, and it tells how to access the full agenda. Finally, it tells you what you must have been sure to do if you decide to sue the City. It connects you directly to the City Manager for more information or assistance.

CITY OF GROVER BEACH
NOTICE OF PUBLIC HEARING

NOTICE IS HEREBY GIVEN that the City Council of the City of Grover Beach will conduct a Public Hearing at **6:00 p.m.**, or soon thereafter, on **Monday, July 26, 2021** to consider the following item:

Meetings can be viewed on Channel 20 and are live streamed on the City's website and on www.slo-span.org. Members of the public may provide public comment during the meeting by calling (805) 321-6639 to provide public comment via phone (the phone line will open just prior to the start of the meeting at 6:00 PM) or written public comments can be submitted via email to *gbadmin@groverbeach.org* prior to the Council meeting no later than 3:00 PM. If submitting written comments in advance of the meeting, please note the agenda item. Written comments will be read out loud during the City Council meeting on the appropriate agenda item subject to the customary 3-minute time limit.

<u>SUBJECT</u>:

1. **Council District Elections** –The City Council will conduct a public hearing to receive public input regarding the composition of potential Council election district boundaries. Following the public hearings, draft maps of potential Council election district boundaries will be published, and additional public hearings scheduled.

Where You Come In:
Any member of the public may appear at the meeting and be heard on the item described in this notice or submit written comments to the City Clerk prior to the meeting by personal delivery or by mail to: City Clerk's Office, 154 South Eighth Street, Grover Beach, CA 93433 or by email to *gbadmin@groverbeach.org*. If you require special accommodations to participate in the public hearing, please contact the City Clerk's office at least 48 hours in advance of the meeting by calling (805) 473-4567.

For More Information:
If you have any questions or would like more information regarding the item described in this notice, please contact: City Manager Matthew Bronson by telephone at (805) 473-4567 or send an email to *mbronson@groverbeach.org*.

The City Council may also discuss other hearings or items of business at this meeting. The complete meeting agenda and copy of the staff report on the above item will be posted on the city website at *www.groverbeach.org*. Live broadcasts of City Council meetings may be seen on cable television Channel 20, as well as over the Internet at *www.groverbeach.org* (click on the icon "Government Access Local Channel 20" and then "Channel 20"). City Council meetings are rebroadcast throughout the week.

If you challenge the nature of the proposed action in court, you may be limited to raising only those issues you or someone else raised at the Public Hearing(s) described in this notice, or in written correspondence delivered to the City at, or prior to, the Public Hearing (Govt. Code Sec 65009).

/s/ Wendi Sims, City Clerk
Dated: Thursday, July 15, 2021

<u>Publish</u>: 1x – *The New Times* on Thurs, July 15, 2021
<u>Post</u>: Grover Beach City Hall

The agenda that follows is the PDF version that is linked from the online version shown at the beginning of the chapter. It is very thorough with all the information needed for the process and for participation. It explains how things will be done. Unfortunately, most people don't read the small print, and many people won't have a handle on it the first time through even if they do read it. As a new Councilmember it is important to familiarize yourself with the small print.

AGENDA
GROVER BEACH CITY COUNCIL
GROVER BEACH CITY HALL - COUNCIL CHAMBER
154 SOUTH EIGHTH STREET
GROVER BEACH, CALIFORNIA
MONDAY, NOVEMBER 4, 2019, 6:00 PM

*Next Resolution No. **19-55***
*Next Ordinance No. **19-11***

In compliance with the Americans with Disabilities Act, if you need special assistance to participate in a City meeting, please contact the City Clerk's Office (805-473-4567) at least 48 hours prior to the meeting to ensure that reasonable arrangements can be made to provide accessibility to the meeting.

PLEASE SUBMIT ALL CORRESPONDENCE FOR CITY COUNCIL *PRIOR*
TO THE MEETING WITH A COPY TO THE CITY CLERK

City Council meetings are webcast live on the City website at *www.groverbeach.org* and broadcast live on Charter Cable Television's Government Access Channel 20. Re-broadcasts are daily at 1:00 a.m., 9:00 a.m., and 6:00 p.m. the week of the meeting, and Thursdays and Sundays at 1:00 a.m., 9:00 a.m., and 6:00 p.m. the week following the meeting.

CALL TO ORDER

MOMENT OF SILENCE

FLAG SALUTE

ROLL CALL Council Members Karen Bright, Desi Lance, and Barbara Nicolls, Mayor Pro Tem Mariam Shah, and Mayor Jeff Lee

CLOSED SESSION ANNOUNCEMENTS

None

AGENDA REVIEW

At this time the City Council will review the order of business to be conducted and receive requests for, or make announcements regarding, any change(s) in the order of the day. The Council should by motion adopt the agenda as presented or as revised.

CEREMONIAL CALENDAR

1.   Proclamation for **National Hospice Palliative Care Month**

PUBLIC COMMUNICATIONS

During this time, the Council will allow up to 15 minutes for Public Communication with additional communication, if necessary, allowed after the Regular Business Items. Any member of the public may address the Council for a period not to exceed three minutes total on any item of interest within the jurisdiction of this Council. The Council will listen to all communications; however, in compliance with the Brown Act, the Council cannot act on items not on the agenda.

<u>CONSENT AGENDA</u>

The following routine items listed below are scheduled for consideration as a group. Recommendations for each item are noted in parentheses. Members of the audience may speak on any item(s) listed on the Consent Agenda. Any Council Member, the City Attorney, or the City Manager may request that an item be withdrawn from the Consent Agenda to allow for full discussion. Items withdrawn from the Consent Agenda will be heard after the rest of the Consent Agenda is approved.

2. **Minutes of the City Council Meeting on Monday, October 21, 2019.**
   (**<u>Recommended Action</u>**: Approved the minutes as submitted or revised.)
   VOICE VOTE

3. **Professional Services Agreement for a Senior Center Feasibility Study** – Community Development Director Buckingham The City Council will consider a Professional Service Agreement for a senior center feasibility study.
   (**Recommended Action**: Approve a Professional Services Agreement with GreenPlay, LLC for preparation of a senior center feasibility study and authorize the City Manager to execute this agreement on behalf of the City.)
   ROLL CALL VOTE

4. **Resolution to Submit an Application for the SB 2 Planning Grants Program** – Community Development Director Buckingham The City Council will consider a Resolution to submit an application for SB 2 Planning Grant Funds.
   (**Recommended Action:** Adopt a Resolution authorizing the City Manager to submit an application for SB 2 Planning Grant Funds to accelerate housing production and execute any agreements necessary for the use of grant funds.)
   ROLL CALL VOTE

5. **Award of Construction Contract Measure K-14 Street Improvements CIP 2295-9, S. 16th Street** – Public Works Director/City Engineer Ray and CIP Manager Wiggin
   (**Recommended Action:** Award the contract for construction of CIP 2295-9 as part of the Measure K-14 Street Rehabilitation Program to CalPortland Construction, in the amount of $394,676.00 for the Base Bid; authorize the City Manager to sign and affirm construction and construction management change orders up to an aggregate of $59,200.00 and authorize the Mayor to execute the contract on behalf of the City).
   ROLL CALL VOTE

6. **Community Development Block Grant (CDBG) Water Main Project (CIP 4267 - 2020): Award of Professional Design Engineering Services** – Public Works Director/City Engineer Ray and CIP Manager Wiggin The City Council will consider a Professional Service Agreement for Design Engineering services for the CDBG Water Main Project CIP 4267.
   (**Recommended Action:** Approve a Professional Services Agreement with MKN & Associates for design services associated with the CIP 4267-2020 CDBG Water Main Project and authorize the Mayor to execute the agreement on behalf of the City.)

PUBLIC HEARING

7. **Introduction and First Reading of an Ordinance to Amend Municipal Code Article VIII Building Regulations Chapter 1 to Adopt by Reference the 2019 California Building Codes and 2018 International Property Maintenance Code with Local Amendments** – Community Development Director Buckingham & Fire Chief Lieberman
    The City Council will conduct an introduction and first reading of an Ordinance to Amend the Grover Beach Municipal Code Article VIII, Chapter 1 in regards to Building Regulations.
    (**Recommended Action:**
    1) Introduce the Ordinance to amend Grover Beach Municipal Code Article VIII Building Regulations Chapter 1 to adopt the 2019 California Building Codes and the 2018 International Property Maintenance Code with local amendments;
    2) Adopt a resolution setting forth the findings required by the California Health and Safety Code to support local amendments; and
    3) Schedule the second reading and adoption at the next regularly scheduled City Council meeting.)
    ROLL CALL VOTE

REGULAR BUSINESS

8. **Economic Development Activities** – City Manager Bronson The City Council will receive information on the City's economic development activities.
    (**Recommended Actions:** Receive information on the City's economic development activities as identified in the 2019-21 Major City Goals work program and 2017 Economic Development Strategy and provide input and direction to staff

9. **Monterey Bay Community Power Policy Board Memorandum of Understanding** – City Manager Bronson The City Council will consider a Memorandum of Understanding regarding a shared Board seat on the Monterey Bay Community Power Joint Powers Authority.
    (**Recommended Actions:** Approve a Memorandum of Understanding regarding the shared Board seat between the City of Grover Beach, City of Arroyo Grande, and City of Pismo Beach on the Monterey Bay Community Power Joint Powers Authority Policy Board and select the City's representative to fill the initial two-year term of this seat.)

PUBLIC COMMUNICATIONS

Any member of the public may address the Council for a period not to exceed three minutes total on any item of interest within the jurisdiction of this Council. The Council will listen to all communications; however, in compliance with the Brown Act, the Council cannot act on items not on the agenda.

COUNCIL COMMITTEE REPORTS

This item gives the Mayor and Council Members the opportunity to present reports to the other members regarding committees, commissions, boards, or special projects on which they may be participating.

Integrated Waste Management Authority (IWMA)	Jeff Lee (Alt: Karen Bright)
Regional Groundwater Sustainability Project (RGSP)	Jeff Lee (Alt: Mariam Shah)
SLO Council of Governments / SLO Regional Transit Authority (SLOCOG / SLORTA)	Jeff Lee (Alt: Mariam Shah)
South SLO County Sanitation District (SSLOCSD)	Jeff Lee (Alt: Barbara Nicolls)
Air Pollution Control District (APCD)	Mariam Shah (Alt: Barbara Nicolls)

Homeless Services Oversight Council (HSOC)	Mariam Shah (Alt: Desi Lance)
Visit San Luis Obispo County	Mariam Shah (Alt: Karen Bright)
Economic Vitality Corporation (EVC)	Karen Bright (Alt: Barbara Nicolls)
SLO Coastal Regional Sediment Management Plan (CRSMP) Steering Committee	Karen Bright (Alt: Jeff Lee)
Zone Three Advisory Committee	Karen Bright (Alt: Desi Lance)
SLO County Water Resources Advisory Committee (WRAC)	Desi Lance (Alt: Karen Bright)
Five Cities Fire Joint Powers Authority	Barbara Nicolls (Alt: Karen Bright)
South County Chambers of Commerce	Barbara Nicolls (Alt: Desi Lance)
South County Transit (SCT)	Barbara Nicolls (Alt: Desi Lance)

League of California Cities - Policy Committee Reports and Other League Matters

Channel Counties Division	Mariam Shah
Transportation, Communication & Public Works Policy Committee	Jeff Lee
Governance, Transparency & Labor Relations Policy Committee	Matthew Bronson

COUNCIL COMMUNICATIONS

This item gives individual Council Members the opportunity to seek consensus for scheduling a specific item on a future agenda, authorizing staff time to provide background information and prepare a staff report for a future agenda, or to comment on Council business, City operations, projects or other items of community interest.

CITY MANAGER'S REPORTS AND COMMENTS

CITY ATTORNEY'S REPORTS AND COMMENTS

CLOSED SESSION

None

ADJOURNMENT

Per Resolution No. 17-21, the public portion of City Council meetings will be scheduled to start at 6:00 p.m. and conclude no later than 11:00 p.m. Any open session items remaining on the agenda at 11:00 p.m. that have not been discussed or considered by the City Council will be continued to an adjourned meeting of the City Council (scheduled before the next regular meeting). However, the City Council may choose to continue the meeting past 11:00 p.m. upon a proper motion and a 4/5ths vote in favor of such an action.

Staff reports or other written materials relating to each item of business referred to on this agenda are available from the City website *www.groverbeach.org* and on file in the City Clerk's Office. A public counter copy is available for public inspection and reproduction during normal business hours at City Hall, 154 South 8th Street, Grover Beach, CA. Related materials submitted after distribution of the agenda packet are available in the City Clerk's Office during normal business hours. If you have questions regarding any agenda item, please contact the appropriate City Department. Any writings or documents regarding any item on this agenda, not exempt from public disclosure, provided to a majority of the City Council and distributed subsequent to distribution of the agenda packet will be made available for public inspection in the City Clerk's Office during normal business hours.

Note: This agenda was prepared and posted pursuant to Government Code Section 54954.2. This agenda is subject to amendment up to 72 hours prior to the date and time set for the meeting. Please refer to the agenda posted at City Hall for any revisions or call the City Clerk's Office at (805) 473-4567 for more information.

The consent agenda items on this agenda are all reasonable, except for number 5. The approval of almost $400,000 for street improvements that will be paid for by a bond that will increase property taxes. An item of this cost relative to the City's overall budget and which will affect people's disposable income should come under the regular business heading, not the consent agenda. That feels sneaky. However, the agenda states that the public may speak on consent agenda items, which although not required by law, is a good practice.

On this agenda there is a second opportunity for Public Communications, presumably any that did not fit into the 15 minutes allocated at the beginning of the meeting. I am disappointed to see that, while it is legal, the public communication period is limited and then tacked on at the end of the meeting. While it might allow latecomers to get in on time to make a comment, the action seems sneaky to me. It means anyone who couldn't squeeze into the first 15 minutes (only 5 commenters at 3 minutes each) has to endure the whole meeting before being allowed to raise an issue.

The information following the **Adjournment** is useful and good practice.

Paragraph 1, the **Decorum** section, is well written and well explained. Two paragraphs, however, contain blatant **First Amendment** and **Brown Act** violations, the important principle being that we must be free to criticize our government. Paragraph 1 restricts the right of a Councilmember to criticize a fellow Councilmember. Paragraph 3 restricts the right of the public to make, "personal, impertinent, slanderous, or profane remarks," threatening them with forceable removal if they do so. The Brown Act, 54954.3. (c) states that "the legislative body of a local agency shall not prohibit public criticism of the policies, procedures, programs, or services of the agency, or of the acts or omissions of the legislative body."

As my friend, the constitutional attorney says, "There's a reason the First Amendment is the FIRST amendment in both our State and national Constitutions!" It is the most important. That reason has a lot to do with the tyranny the founding fathers were escaping when forming our country.

They were seeking freedom from rulers who gave them no say in their taxes, no religious freedom, no ability to speak their truth.

In government meetings you cannot tell people how to behave. You can only curb behavior that disrupts the process. This is an area where people often confuse the amendment's application, thinking that it applies universally to all situations in the United States. This is not so. It applies to the government.

The first amendment protects us from a *government* that would not allow these rights. Unlike government institutions, private organizations (unless they receive government funding) MAY abridge speech. The government cannot tell us how we may and may not speak to government and what we may or may not say. Private organizations CAN make rules governing etiquette in their meetings. In non-government settings we do not have freedom of speech. Twitter and Facebook CAN set rules for engagement, even cut you off. Your government cannot. The Rotary Club CAN ban language they don't like. The government cannot.

While it is constructive to advocate for standards of communication for the Council and staff that enhance good communication, it may not be defensible to demand it because government employees and elected officials also have the first amendment right to free speech. While Councilmembers and staff should set an example of professional effective public discourse and certainly will set the tone of the meeting, nothing can take away their right to free speech in a government setting.

There is another principle involved, unrelated to the above. I believed to be true, and found it to be refreshingly so, that when you allow people to express themselves and they are genuinely heard, it changes the discourse from confrontational to conversational and constructive. Enemies can become friends. Solutions can be mutually agreed.

NOTES

CITY OF GROVER BEACH
POLICIES AND PROCEDURES FOR CONDUCT AND DECORUM AT COUNCIL MEETINGS
(Pursuant to Resolution No. 07-44, adopted 04-16-07)

1.0   DECORUM AND ORDER – COUNCIL MEMBERS

Council Members shall accord the utmost courtesy to each other, to administrative staff and to the public appearing before the City Council and shall refrain at all times from rude, abusive, and/or derogatory remarks or those that reflect upon a person's integrity, motives or personality.

2.0   DECORUM AND ORDER – STAFF

2.1   <u>City Manager Responsibilities</u>
The City Manager is responsible for ensuring that members of the administrative staff observe the rules of decorum and order set forth in this Policy.

2.2   <u>Addressing the City Council</u>
Any administrative staff member desiring to address the City Council or members of the public shall first be recognized by the Mayor/Presiding Officer. All remarks shall be addressed to the Mayor/Presiding Officer and not to any individual Council Member or member of the public. Administrative staff members shall accord the utmost courtesy to the City Council, other administrative staff members and the public.

3.0   DECORUM AND ORDER – MEMBERS OF THE PUBLIC

3.1   <u>Addressing the City Council</u>
Any member of the public desiring to address the City Council or members of the public shall first be recognized by the Mayor/Presiding Officer at the appropriate place on the agenda. All remarks shall be addressed to the Mayor/Presiding Officer and not to any individual Council Member, member of the administrative staff or member of the public.

3.2   <u>Time limitation for addressing the City Council</u>
Public comment when addressing the City Council shall be generally limited to three (3) minutes per speaker. Depending on the extent of the agenda and the number of persons desiring to speak on an issue, the Mayor/Presiding Officer may, at the beginning of the hearing, set a different time limit for each speaker. Any person may speak for a longer period of time upon approval from the Mayor/Presiding Officer, when deemed necessary, for instance when a person is speaking on behalf of a group, or has a graphic or slide presentation requiring more time.

3.3   <u>Removal</u>
Any member of the public making personal, impertinent, and slanderous or profane remarks or who becomes boisterous while addressing the City Council, staff or general public or while attending the City Council meeting and refuses to come to order at the direction of the Mayor/Presiding Officer, shall be removed from the Council Chambers by the sergeant-at-arms and may be barred from further attendance before the Council during that meeting. Unauthorized remarks from the audience, stamping of feet, whistles, yells, and similar demonstrations shall not be permitted by the Mayor/Presiding Officer. The Mayor/Presiding Officer may direct the sergeant-at-arms to remove such offenders from the room.[1]

3.4   <u>Prosecution</u>
Aggravated cases shall be prosecuted on appropriate complaint signed by the Mayor/Presiding Officer.

4.0   ENFORCEMENT OF DECORUM

In extreme cases, such as when a meeting is willfully interrupted by a group or groups of persons so as to render the orderly conduct of such meeting unfeasible and order cannot be restored by the removal of individuals as provided for in this Policy, the Mayor/Presiding Officer may order the meeting room cleared and continue in session. Only matters appearing on the agenda may be considered in such a session. Duly accredited representatives of the press or other news media, except those participating in the disturbance, shall be allowed to attend any session held pursuant to this Section. Nothing in this Section shall prohibit the City Council from establishing a procedure for readmitting an individual or individuals not responsible for willfully disturbing the orderly conduct of the meeting.

Unfortunately, the excellent, welcoming opening in the Notice of Meetings and the excellent explanations of how to participate are lost in the later restrictions that thwart public participation and free speech. These include public speaking restricted to 15 minutes then continued at the end of a meeting, not putting a large expenditure on the regular agenda, and telling people they can only speak in certain ways.

At this point we have worked our way through the agenda and the fine print, so let's take a look at the agenda packet. Next is an example of a brief City Council **Staff Report.** The report starts well, explaining the history, but does not finish well. It would have been helpful to hear what neighboring Cities and communities and agencies are doing, especially considering that the agencies nearby always work together in matters of public safety and especially in instances that might require the use of military supplies. How can they work together if they all have different Military Use Policies? There should be consistency in governance especially when governments assist one another in public safety! This is very bad practice. It is a good concise report, but especially as it is an 'urgent' ordinance, the actions of neighboring Cities should have been included, or an explanation provided as to why they are not. This could be an instance of something looking bad that is not—perhaps ours is the first and will be the pro forma for all local Cities, or perhaps they are all the same; or perhaps we are the only City with this equipment. This may be a good example of why it is important to ask questions. Sometimes they turn up an answer that all is well except for a simple matter of communication that can be improved in future Staff reports.

CITY COUNCIL STAFF REPORT

TO: Honorable Mayor and City Council   **DATE:** March 14, 2022

FROM: Matthew Bronson, City Manager

PREPARED BY: Jim Munro, Commander
John Peters, Chief of Police

SUBJECT: Urgency Ordinance Adopting a Military Equipment Use Policy in Accordance with Assembly Bill No. 481

RECOMMENDATION

Adopt an Urgency Ordinance establishing a Military Equipment Use Policy in accordance with California Assembly Bill No. 481 and in compliance with California Government Code Section 7071.

BACKGROUND

On September 30, 2021, Governor Gavin Newsom signed Assembly Bill 481 into law adding Chapter 12.8, Sections 7070 through 7075 to Division 7 of Title 1 of the Government Code. This new legislation requires that by May 1, 2022, all law enforcement agencies "shall obtain approval from their governing body, via adoption of a military equipment use policy by ordinance prior to the law enforcement agency funding, acquiring, or using equipment identified as military equipment. Staff would emphasize that the term "military equipment", as used in AB 481, does not necessarily indicate equipment that has been used by the military.

Pursuant to AB 481, equipment deemed to be "military equipment" includes, but is not limited to, unmanned aerial or ground vehicles, armored vehicles, command and control vehicles, pepper balls, less lethal shotguns, less lethal 40mm projectile launchers, long range acoustic devices, and flashbang distraction devices. The Police Department is committed to using the most up-to-date equipment to safeguard the community. Many of the items deemed "military equipment" by AB 481 are in fact already deployed by the Police Department and many other law enforcement agencies across the country in order to specifically reduce the risk to the community and officers. This equipment helps officers to safely resolve volatile incidents which otherwise might result in a lethal force encounter.

Staff has prepared a draft Military Equipment Use Policy with a list of the current equipment used by the Police Department (Attachment 1, Exhibit A) and prepared an Urgency Ordinance (Attachment 1) for Council's consideration. Staff is bringing this to the Council as an Urgency Ordinance with an immediate effective date as the City is planning to take ownership of a new mobile command vehicle in late March 2022 with a separate agenda item during this meeting for the lease payment of this vehicle. Such a vehicle is defined as "military equipment" which requires the immediate implementation of this Ordinance.

Staff conducted a community engagement meeting on January 26, 2022, to discuss AB 481 and the equipment used by the Police Department. Staff also posted the draft documents on the Police Department's website for community review. Staff has not received any public comments in

The Fab Four Public Meeting Sunshine Violations:

It's very easy, in the heat of a meeting, to lose track of where you are. If any of the following begin to arise, it is your duty to raise a "point of order" with the Chair. Usually, the chair or agency attorney will catch it first.

1. Councilmembers express views before hearing public opinion

2. Councilmembers go off on a tangent discussing items not on the agenda

3. Councilmembers, when discussing whether or not to agendize an item stray into a discussion of the merits of the item rather than agendizing it before discussing it

4. Agenda items are misidentified or positioned on the agenda in such a way as to avoid public scrutiny

NOTES

____

____

____

____

____

____

____

____

____

PART 3

Boardsmanship

"Government almost never polices itself. When government agencies lose money, or fail at their missions, they ask Congress for more money. They usually get it, citing their failure to achieve their goals as proof that they need more funds." –John Stossel, Co-Anchor of ABC's 20/20

 # HAVING YOUR SAY—STAGE PRESENCE

Vocabulary

Grandstanding	Drawing attention to yourself rather than the matter at hand

Sometimes it ain't what you say, it's the way that you say it. Sometimes no matter how you say it, it won't work.

Public meetings are live, videotaped and preserved. Like anything else, how you look, how you dress, how you speak and present yourself, does influence whether or not you are listened to and considered credible. Aretha Franklin had it right in her 1960's hit, *R-E-S-P-E-C-T*. The importance of the office and the government we create is best demonstrated by dressing and addressing one another respectfully. It can determine the success or failure of your message.

A friend recently gave a campaign speech. His speech was excellent on paper. His delivery was dreadful. He dressed in baggy shorts, a baggy shirt, and his hair was unkempt. He spoke in a monotone too quiet to be heard and sounded unsure of himself. Although he was an incumbent Board member who had served the association well as the chair of the security committee, he didn't get voted back onto the Board.

On that same Board are two knowledgeable, competent women who have also selflessly served the association. Both have an abrupt manner of speaking and do not suffer fools. Their hearts are in the right place, but their manner rubs people the wrong way and polarizes, rather than creating consensus. It has caused and exacerbated many unnecessary conflicts, not just for them, but also for fellow Board members.

Here are some tips that will help you more successfully garner the ear of others when speaking in a government setting.

From the dais:

- A hack—provided you never have to rise from the dais, what you wear on your bottom half matters much less than what you wear on the top half.

- NEVER roll your eyes, look bored, or say anything you wouldn't say publicly—microphones sometimes stay live, and videotaped or Zoom meetings are posted indefinitely and can be downloaded and retained for a very long time. You may eventually regret it.

- Speak courteously and respectfully to fellow Councilmembers, staff, and speakers. Thank them for participating.

- Don't use government jargon or acronyms. Speak in plain language that everyone can understand. Say the words associated with the letters of acronyms so the public can understand and follow the information presented.

- If you have something to say on a matter, speak up quickly, or the chair will move on, and you will miss your opportunity.

- If you share a view previously voiced, just say so. Don't waste everyone's time repeating it unless it could be said better.

- No matter how passionate, upset, or annoyed you are, unless you don't care about the outcome and just want to blow off steam, make your comments respectful. Think of it as a poker game. Do not show your feelings unless you intend to do so. Here's how I think of it: "Nobody else gets to determine my response. Only I do that."

- Be sure that your comments are about something within the purview of the agency or relevant to the agenda item. Don't **grandstand**. A good chairperson will cut you off if you are headed in that direction.

- Come prepared to speak, but don't write a speech that you read verbatim.

- Address Councilmembers and staff by their formal titles, i.e., Mayor, Councilmember, City Manager, City Attorney.

- Humor (but not at someone's expense) is appreciated.

- Review how you did and how you can do better next time. Ask others for helpful feedback. If criticism would dissuade you from trying again, ask specific questions that won't leave you dispirited, i.e., "Should I have worn a different color?" or "Did I speak too quickly?"

TIP: You can ask that your message be included in the public record with the minutes.

NOTES

____

____

____

____

____

____

____

____

 # CHECKS AND BALANCES

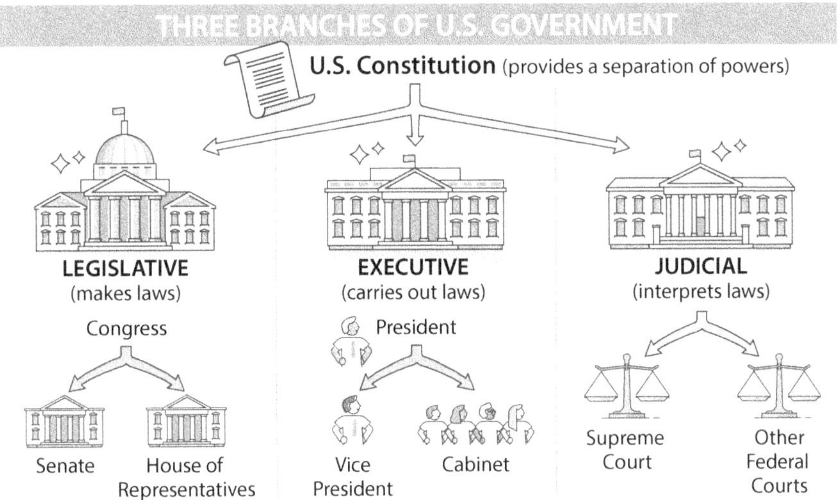

There is nowhere that checks and balances are more important than in managing the funds we provide to our public servants to provide essential services for our safety and wellbeing. Our government was envisioned as one in which our elected representatives would step aside from their daily professions for a time to serve and then return to them. It is still the case that both our elected officials and those they appoint change office often, in which case there is no institutional memory and no consistency of oversight from term to term. For this reason, it is critical that good systems be in place to protect the public, the owners of the institutions, and to ensure the highest level of integrity of those we elect to oversee our affairs.

The three branches of the United States Government and our State Governments are:

- **Legislative**—Make the laws
  - Congress
  - Senate
  - House of Representatives

- **Executive**—Carry out the laws
  - President
  - Vice President
  - Cabinet

- **Judicial**—Interprets the laws
  - Supreme Court
  - Other Federal Courts

The three branches of government in the United States are often referred to as the "three estates" devised so that no one estate can take the others over.

Most U.S. citizens recall being taught in school that we are a nation of checks and balances; that our government is set up with three branches, each being equal to, and balancing the others, so that no one estate may overtake the other. The Legislative branch (Congress) makes the laws. The Executive (The President & Vice President) enforces the laws, and the Judicial (the Courts) interprets the laws.

Therefore, as citizens we expect that we can rely on the system to police itself. At the local level, the checks and balances of the federal and State level do not exist. The branches are a hierarchy with the executive stacked beneath the City Council and the Judicial off to one side at a higher level of government.

Only the Legislative branch—The City Council—is elected—performing the function of both the House of Representatives and Senate. The Executive branch—those who carry out the laws—equivalent to the President & Vice President—are appointed by the City Council (City Manager). In turn, the City Manager appoints department heads and the Chief of Police. The Council appoints the City Attorney. There is no local Judicial branch. At County, City, and District levels, checks and balances move out of the hands of The People and into the hands of elected Councils and Board Members. The District Attorney and Sheriff are elected at County level. If the City Manager and City Attorney were elected posts, the chart above would look much more like the chart at the national level; the one we recognize as best governance. At District level, voter control is even further diluted because District Boards are made up of representatives from City Councils and Boards of Supervisors. Thus, the critical job of oversight depends on the integrity of the Councils and Boards, staff, and The People they serve. For this reason, knowledge of Board roles and responsibilities is critical.

Exercise: Draw an organizational chart for your City, laying out the hierarchy. Mine looks like the one below. What does yours look like?

Label the three branches of government:

Legislative, Executive, Judicial

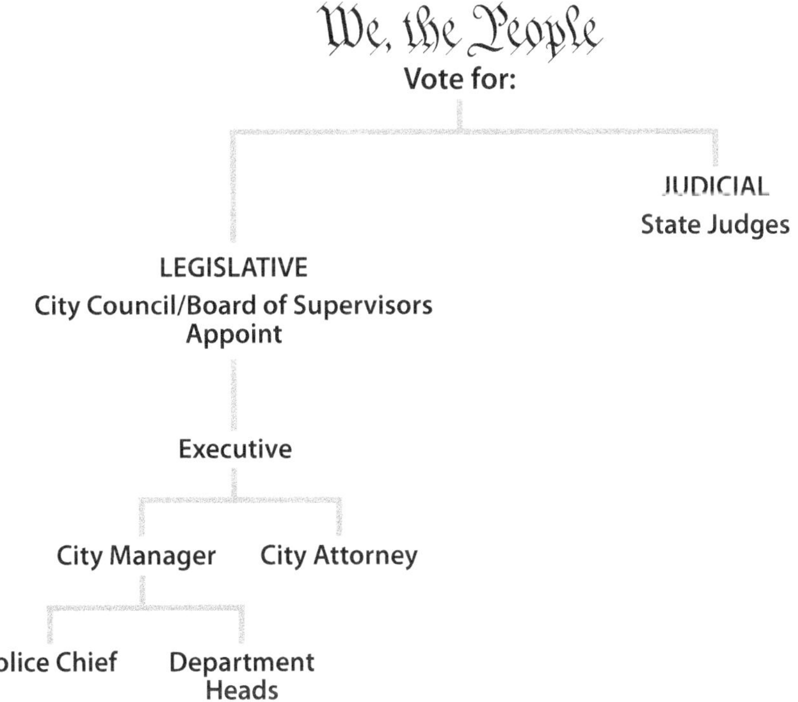

We, the People

NO BRANCHES OF
LOCAL GOVERNMENT

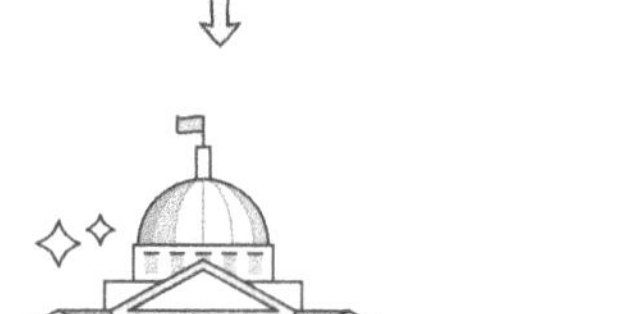

State Constitution
(provides no separation
of powers)

JUDICIAL
(interprets laws)

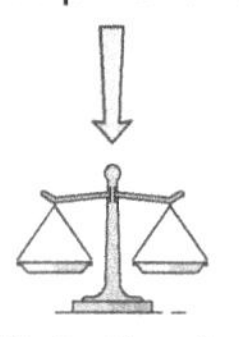

State Courts

CITY COUNCIL /
BOARD OF SUPERVISORS
(Legislative)

CEO & ATTORNEYS
(Executive)
City Manager
City
Attorney

Police
Chief
Department
Heads

At the County, City, and District level, the basic safeguards of accountability have been abandoned. This is part of the reason that we saw so many corrupt government machines at the turn of the twentieth century and why we continue to see corruption at the local level. At the District level, enforcement is often carried out by outside consultants. Accordingly, it reinforces the importance of additional involvement by other estates at the local level.

We believe that our only job is to vote. That teaching, which is correct as far as our Constitution is concerned, applies to the nation and to our States. We think of our Cities and local Districts as part of this system of government that is protected by the balance of these three estates.

Although our forebears envisioned American citizens as active participants in their government, there is no proactive teaching about the role of citizens in the care of their government institutions. Our role as citizens was widely discussed at the time our Constitution was created and is broadly protected in the Constitution, but the directives to us to oversee our government seem to be presumed rather than articulated in the Constitution.

The longest standing written Constitution, from which our own Constitution, and by extension, the United Nations Charter, were derived is the Iroquois [pronounced ee·ruh·kwaa] Confederacy Great Law of Peace, first recorded in the 12th Century and now embraced by native tribal nations worldwide. George Washington, Ben Franklin, and Thomas Jefferson met frequently with the Iroquois and became familiar with the Great Law of Peace, acknowledged December 2, 1987, in U.S. Senate Resolution 76.

Several delegates from the Iroquois Confederacy attended the Continental Congress in 1776 when the Declaration of Independence was written, and the Constitution of the United States was drafted.

The Iroquois say that our founding fathers copied the Great Law of Peace but didn't really understand it because they left out two essential principles: the 7th Generation and Women in Leadership. It took another 150 years before women were allowed to vote. Even today women in political office make up much less than their share of the population in the United States. Native Americans teach that we must consider how every decision will affect our descendants seven Lakota generations into the future (seven hundred years). I agree with their best principles of women in office and consideration of future generations in decision-making.

Herein are two tips for best Boardsmanship. On government Boards—elect and appoint more women and consider the effects of your decisions seven generations hence if you want more peace. Statistically, Boards run by women are more financially sound. The old boys' club does not bind women because they do not understand it and have never been members. They are left to deal in the truth more freely and with a greater connection to their communities' needs.

Welcome diversity of opinion, engage in spirited discourse. Challenge groupthink because it kills creative problem-solving.

Now comes the mentoring on Boardsmanship that I received from the chairman of an international bank. What do you think he said is the number one most important thing a good Board member must do? "ASK QUESTIONS!" He gave me examples of how to spot red flags in financial reports and what questions Board members should ask in order to uphold their fiscal obligation to protect their institutions.

Over the years I have learned many more that apply in a local government setting. I am going to pass these on to you in the Red Flags Roll—things that you must question if you see them. A lack of interest in pursuit of these red flags by other Board members is, in fact, also a red flag!

 # RED FLAGS, SNEAKY TRICKS, & 22 SIGNS OF THE CRIMES

VOCABULARY

Emoto-Cons	Chief Executives that draw attention away from the real problem with displays of emotion. CEmO.
Weasel Words	
Acronyms	

We have huge influence and huge responsibility for the day to day lives of The People in our communities. It is therefore critical that we carefully oversee the work of those who manage the work of the City on a day-to-day basis. The voters will hold us accountable for the success or failure of how we hold our institutions accountable.

First and foremost, my mentor said that things should be easily understood and should pass the smell test. If not, question until we understand and they smell good, or staff make the necessary changes so that the information is clear. The following are red flags that must be queried:

1. Multiple lawsuits or a legal budget that is out of sync with the budgets of other agencies of similar size and remit

2. High Staff Turnover

3. Opacity (as opposed to transparency)

4. Violations of statutory reporting requirements and permissions

5. Counsel works for the Chief Executive (not the Board, and not The People); for example, writing contracts that favor the Chief Executive or suppliers, rather than the agency and The People

6. Open government violations

7. Attitude that there is always more money, or that the solution to problems is to just raise taxes

8. Resistance to providing information

9. Manipulative CEO. (Emoto-Cons) Manipulates by hijacking your emotions, so you are so focused on the emotional content that you do not think clearly about the subject matter but try to solve the emotional crisis; turns off your executive brain: the whiner, the charmer, the temptress who redirects your thinking so that you do not analyze the subject matter

10. Eschews best practice, such as attaching metrics to goals, reviewing projects to evaluate effectiveness, and periodic departmental audits

11. Disregard for usual and customary good business and accounting practices

12. Frames things in a way to make opponents feel or appear stupid for arguing with them

13. Seeks to humiliate those who question

14. Denigrate others rather than exploring alternative points of view

15. Delayed or absent annual audits and reviews of executive staff, counsel, and programs

16. Culture of fear: staff and the public fear reprisals

17. Outward signs of increasing wealth or high expense addictive behavior— gambling, horse bets, alcohol, cocaine, sex trafficking, partying

18. Staff reports do not provide information as to how the issue being reported on is addressed by nearby or similar agencies (consistency in governance)

19. Staff reports do not provide alternative solutions, only staff's recommendation

20. Counsel is too cozy with staff

21. CEO has too much power. Answers to no one. No legitimate appeal process against CEO actions

22. Public are afraid to question agency because of its unchecked power to fine.

23. Response to questions is defensive as opposed to informative or considered

24. CEO is "God" and mustn't be questioned

25. Response to questions: baffle with science, talk in circles, techno-speak, claim not to have the information on hand. If someone disagrees, say it's incorrect and pick out a technicality to deny, offer assurances that of course everything will be done fairly, and everything is OK because everybody loves us or "we are all good people"

26. Derisive attitude to Board members and public

27. CEO goes out on his own with published editorial viewpoints, press releases and presentations before presenting to or without notifying the Board

28. Infrequent Board meetings, making consistent oversight impossible

29. Constant whining or blaming someone else for lack of forward progress "Oh we've spent SOOOOO much time on this that there's not enough time to do our jobs"

30. Never completes investigations or projects

31. Don't address the real issues in reports

32. Don't enforce resolutions and ordinances

33. Deselect facts that do not support their position

34. Failure to disclose

35. Alliances with certain Board members or failure to build good relationships with Board members

36. Information doesn't make sense. Are the difficult areas explained, i.e., is the Public Employee Retirement System (PERS) separately accounted for so voters can see how much goes to retirees and pensions as opposed to the actual operations of the agency and serving the public?

37. Weasel Words

38. ACRONYMS

Exercise: Take a look at your City or a local agency website and look for the budget, or any project including a financial report. Can you understand it? Does it make sense? Do the costs seem reasonable for the job at hand? Are there any red flags? If it doesn't pass the smell test, what are you going to do about it?

Checklist of Sneaky Tricks

I didn't learn of the sneaky "workarounds" until I became a Councilmember when City Managers would propose that a discussion be held in closed session because it was uncomfortable for the Council to discuss it in public. THAT is not an allowable Brown Act reason for holding a conversation in closed session!

The Act is often misused by applying one of the allowed agenda headings to cover a matter that doesn't fit under the heading to hold the very secret meetings it was designed to prevent. What follows is a Checklist of Sneaky Tricks government Boards use to get things out of the public eye.

Unless you refuse to participate in a meeting where any of the following take place, the law will count you as complicit.

- Are special meetings scheduled for less accessible venues, on different days, or times?

- Are controversial topics covered in special meetings, thereby making it more likely that fewer citizens can attend?

- Are Councilmembers (inadvertently or intentionally) signaling their voting intent by asserting views when asked for questions before hearing from the public or by making statements posed as questions?

- Does it seem as if the decision is a foregone conclusion, i.e., the Council is not interested in asking questions or hearing from staff or the public? Are they too hasty to vote? This may signal secret meetings by a Council majority.

- Are there changes to an ordinance on the second reading (at the second hearing/meeting)? New ordinances must have at least two public hearings before being finalized. Material changes necessitate an additional hearing to allow public review. The press, media, and public often don't know this and don't show up for second or third "readings" of the ordinance, leaving the Council free to sneak in whatever changes they wish out of the public eye.

- Are there subcommittees that meet without allowing public participation? Are subcommittees making decisions, or is the Board making the decisions? Who appointed the subcommittees? If not the Board, they are not legal. All committees must be open to the public, and decisions are to be made by the full Board or Council following the report-back of the committee to the larger Board.

- Do Councilmembers have information that hasn't been distributed to the public? Any communication circulated among elected representatives and staff becomes public and must be shared with the public upon request, or if relevant to an agenda item, immediately when it is circulated.

- Do there seem to be a lot of closed session meetings that are classified as human relations or legal matters? Does the Board report the outcome of these meetings?

- Have there been whistleblowers of late? What do they report?

- Have insurance rates increased? Why? Ask for a list of payouts.

- Does there seem to be a group on the Council that always votes as a bloc?

- Does it look like there are payments that are not shown in the budget, or line items that are higher than you would expect?

- Can you understand the agenda item description? Does the agenda description match what is actually discussed, or if it were noticed as to the real topic, would people be protesting? Agenda descriptions should be a brief general description of each item of business to be transacted or discussed at the meeting, including items to be discussed in closed session, not exceeding twenty words.

- What's last on the agenda? Is it something that would arouse a lot of public pushback?

- Are you hearing the excuse, "But no one came to disagree with us"?

- Is the agency enforcing the mitigations it puts in place? In the case of the Cannabis ordinances passed in my City in 2017, as concessions to the environment and public safety concerns, cannabis businesses were required by ordinance, regulation, or resolution to hook up to sewers, to install rooftop solar panels, to reapply annually for permits for staff and licensees or in the event of a change of ownership, to hook up security cameras connected to the police department, and to coordinate tax reporting software with City software. At the time of writing, in 2022, most of these legal requirements remained unfulfilled, without City enforcement action.

- Is money being used where the Council promised it would be used, or as the budget dictates?

- Are the budgets balanced?

Example

Here's an example of the kind of thing you may catch: Even as a Planning Commissioner for four years I didn't understand the internal Planning and Building departmental decision-making process, even though as a real estate broker, Councilmember, and Mayor I was in a better position than most to understand. I still don't understand how the charges for permits are decided. It was frustrating to hear complaints from the public without knowing enough to correct the problems. As I have moved through these positions and back into the general public, applying for Planning permission on my own behalf, I see how much room there is for making the Planning and Building Departments more transparent than they are now; for instance, by offering online explanations of the differences between Building and Planning Departments and their roles in approvals.

Processes and charging are so confusing that any amount of fiddling could occur on higher or lower charges for work accomplished, and no one would be the wiser but the individual making the charges and a Department Supervisor or a Manager. I understand that the Department charges out its time, but how much per job, per employee?

I remember being told that my permit fee was an upfront deposit from which the hours needed to handle my case would be deducted. At the prospect of a refund, the right-brain angel on one shoulder caused me to happily respond, "Oh, you mean, I might get money back?" Then, that little left-brain investigator on the other shoulder kicked in, asking clerical staff, "Have you ever actually given any money back to anyone?"

I got an honest answer, "We do get the accounting for hours spent versus money deposited and sometimes it does indicate a credit." The little investigator poked me again. I asked, "Did you actually ever send anyone any money back if the hours added up to less than their 'deposit'?" Looking around the room and asking other members of staff, they all responded, that no, they don't recall ever issuing any refund checks. I intentionally use indirect language here to protect the honest members of staff. Wouldn't that be a fun public records request and audit!

You may ask, "Debbie, why didn't you pursue it?" Well.... partly time and energy and waiting to see how my own deposit vs. hours spent added up, thinking I would tackle it then. The other reason? Fear that if I chased it up, my application for a permit might become more difficult or even be refused. Indeed, the need for the permit itself, exclusive to me, but not others in the same zoning with the same projects, was perceived by many as "payback" from the City Council for bringing to light allegations of corruption. So why didn't I pursue that? My contractor said it would be cheaper and faster to pay the permit than to hire an attorney and then to drag the matter through the courts. Now doesn't that meet the definition of a racket? The Cambridge dictionary defines a racket as "a dishonest or illegal activity that makes money or a way of making a large unfair profit."

I simply didn't have the energy or time or financial bandwidth to go after it. If I can teach others how to go after the many things I have already championed, I will achieve far more in equipping new Councilmembers to demand excellence from the institutions they serve on behalf of The People they represent.

The following screenshots are from the February 20, 2013 sewer District treasurer's report. If interpreting the staff report was an assignment for **Government-Speak 101** the first Question would be:

QUESTION 1 "WHAT'S MISSING HERE?"

Answer: *This is an example of an apparently thorough report. It explains different bank accounts, what money has come in, that the checks are issued and checked by the County, and why the books don't balance. I would call it 'baffling by informing.'*

But wait,

Do you see how the staff report obfuscates? Let's go line by line.

The total revenue was   + \$171,163

Grover \$\$ previously recognized—How much   + ???

Operating Expenses were   −\$336,277

NON-operating expenses were   <u>−\$136,556</u>

So, unless Grover brought in \$165,114 there was a negative balance for the month. I happen to know that Grover does not bring in that amount. How are they covering the negative balance?

But wait, there's more. What were the NON-operating expenses, and where did they come from?

What about Payroll? It comes from a different bank account. Is it included in the Operating Expenses?

We got FOG (Fat Or Grease) reimbursement from businesses that got the service carried out by the administrator's company, but how much did we pay out for the service from the administrator's company? Is that included in the Operating Expenses?

SOUTH SAN LUIS OBISPO COUNTY
SANITATION DISTRICT

Post Office Box 339, Oceano, California 93475-0339
1600 Aloha Place, Oceano, California 93445-9735
Telephone (805) 489-6666 FAX (805) 489-2765
www.sslocsd.org

TO: Board of Directors
FROM: John L. Wallace, *District Administrator*
DATE: February 20, 2013
SUBJECT: Monthly Financial Review (January 2013)

Overall Monthly Summary

During the month of January, the District earned revenue total revenue of $171,163 of which
$101,447 was received from the City of Arroyo Grande for December sewer service, and
$61,851 was earned for sewer service to OCSD for December. December revenue from the City
of Grover Beach had previously been recognized. For the month of January, $1,971 was earned
for the AT&T cell-tower lease, and $1,308 was earned for brine disposal services. FOG and
WDR reimbursements billed in January totaled $4,229. Interest earned on the District's County
Treasury Pool account for the 2nd Quarter was $357.

District operating expenses totaled $336,277 for the month of January. Non-operating expenses
totaled $136,556.

Local Agency Investment Fund

The balance in the District's LAIF account was $3,103,525 at January 31, 2013.

County of San Luis Obispo Treasury Pool

As of January 31, 2013, the reconciled cash balance with the County of San Luis Obispo
Treasury Pool was $340,230. The County issues the majority of the District's checks, and the
majority of the District's revenues are deposited with this agency. As such, the County provides
'banking services' to the District and provides some accounting documents for internal control
purposes.

To arrive at the reconciled cash balance, differences between the District's cash balance and the
County's are investigated for possible errors. These reconciling items are then applied to the
cash balances to arrive at the reconciled amount. At January 31, 2013, the District's books show
a cash balance of $339,947 including the amount of cash allocated to the Medical
Reimbursement Trust account. The County's statement, however, has a cash balance of
$346,988. The difference of $7,041 is the result of reconciling items which have not yet been
posted into either the District's books or the County's system. The District Bookkeeper will
continue working on fully reconciling these two account balances.

Rabobank Funds

The Local Agency Investment Fund had $3,103,525 in it at 1/31/13. What was it the previous month?

COUNTY OF SLO TREASURY POOL

The County issues the majority of the District's checks, and the majority of the District's revenues are deposited with this agency. Which checks aren't issued by them, and which funds NOT deposited? If not, where are the funds deposited, and what checks are issued outside the treasury pool?

RABOBANK FUNDS

Payroll is being funded by one-time new development builder fees that are intended for long-term capital projects but were being transferred into the payroll bank account to cover payroll. It says as much here, but who would guess?

They have said what is being done, giving the appearance of providing all the relevant information without providing enough to compare month to month, or figure out what the bottom line is, or really determine where the money is coming from and going to. However, they have said what the scam is and gotten the Board to sign off on it. Since no one is the wiser they are able to 1.) cover their backsides (create plausible deniability) 2.) continue with an unbalanced budget, and 3.) fool the Board into compliance and bamboozle the public.

But a diligent public did catch them. The administrator was charged with multiple felony and misdemeanor self-dealing offenses and reached a plea deal of reimbursing a small portion of the plant's losses and a misdemeanor. The accountant went on to get a job at the State and never blew the whistle. The agency attorney "retired" when a fraud investigator showed up. One Board chair who was signing to remove capital funds was made a judge. The other was voted out of office in an historic write-in election. Three out of nine employees turned whistleblower and lost their jobs. The Board made sure to groom sycophants who will cover for them.

22 Signs of the Crimes

One or more of these signs doesn't necessarily indicate malfeasance. Several of the following signs or reports of the same concerns by unrelated sources is a strong indicator. Most people reporting information are sincere, concerned, and dependable insofar as they believe what they report to be correct. Looking at the bigger picture, here are the things I consistently find when malfeasance is present:

1. **Incongruity**—Truth, integrity, open government, and constructive human behavior are congruent. The behavior and reports, written or spoken, by government staff and our elected representatives should not only be consistent, but the source should seek to make it clear and easy to understand. Incongruities in reporting or in the character of individuals are the red flags to follow up. As an example, my son, as a small child had an aversion to those friendly costumed characters you see at children's events who sidle up for a photo op. He said it was scary when someone dressed up as something they are not then tried to hug you. Not only is incongruity a red flag of white-collar crime, but incongruity is also a quick indicator of more physically dangerous crimes. Perception of incongruity is the opposite of "paranoia," as may be claimed by people who don't want to address the incongruity. Paranoia is a fear of what is not real. Intuition alerting to incongruity is the sense of what is present and real but often missed or filtered out. Deeming the calling out of incongruity "paranoia" is the mechanism by which the guilty shut down their accusers, and the general populace sees no evil.

2. **Association**—"Make no mistake about this: 'Bad company is the ruin of good character.'" *1 Corinthians 15:33* Incongruity is a red flag, and conversely, so is congruity. Look at people, their businesses, their associates, their partners. People are drawn to people like themselves. Lack of association is as informative as association. If there is no information online or in social media, it may indicate that someone

has expunged their record or is trying to fly under the radar. Nowadays most people have something out there. If what is out there appears "canned" it may be manufactured to deceive. The Chinese proverb says it well, "Show me who your friends are, and I will show you who you are."

3. **Projection**—What does someone say about you? We project our attributes onto others, expecting others to behave as we do, whether good or bad. Listen to the colleagues who call you sneaky, question your motives or call you a liar. It may give insight into how they operate. In the same way, projecting good attributes onto others often indicates good character but should not be confused with the diversionary weasel phrase 'we're all good people.'

4. **People tell you who they are and what they are doing**—when they project their own actions and attributes onto others, when they are caught off-guard, when they just keep talking, when they are tired, or under the influence of alcohol. A wise friend once counseled me, if someone says to you, 'I'm not a nice person,' believe them or at least do not harbor expectations they will be nice. In a recent meeting the attorney admitted about the $150,000 litigation costs he had led the Board into, "I'd like these court cases to continue because that's how I make my money," a confirmation that he not only had a conflict of interest but exercised the financial conflict of interest in encouraging the Board to stay in court! Another classic example is the quote of a former Clovis, California City Councilmember accused of several counts of government malfeasance, who, projecting his fear while proclaiming his innocence, quoted the *Bible*, "A false witness shall not be unpunished and he that speaketh lies shall not escape." In June 1996, following multiple witness accounts of pay-to-play, and a bevy of charges, the councilman entered "guilty" pleas of Extortion Under Color of Official Right and Obstruction of Justice. The quote he used to argue his innocence in turn condemned him, "A false witness shall not be unpunished and he that speaketh lies shall not escape."

5. **"It was a joke."** Watch for **Weasel Words** – The attorney who said, "I'd like to see these cases continue because that's how I make my money," would likely defend his statement by saying, "I was just joking!" Probably not. The truth is in whatever comment you made that you had to excuse by calling it a joke. And it's not funny anyway.

6. **Interpretation**—Learn the language of political discourse. The truth is there, often understated, spoken quietly. Just as in other spheres, government has its jargon; sometimes it takes the form of a shortcut as in the preponderance of anagrams, other times it is a response intended to deceive or divert attention, delivered as confusing or boring text, buried in the small print, or even as a subtext running in conversations. For example, if the Mayor wants to avoid a touchy subject, he will send it back to staff for further study. Sometimes this is legitimate; sometimes it is a way to stall the conversation or stop it altogether without appearing to do so, or the machine boss directive, "Who will rid me of … ?" or "So and So is a real problem."

7. **Context**—When seeking to understand the actions of individuals or Boards, consider the wider context—the big picture, countywide, statewide, nationally, to understand how circumstances drive their decision-making or statements.

8. **Patterns**—Patterns of behavior or speech can betray a source or confirm an activity or relationship. When a pattern of speech or behavior is effective, it is repeated over and over. You can identify associated parties by their speech patterns, tone of voice, mannerisms, terminology, delivery, or by hearing the same story from informants or victims. I remember my skin crawling when I listened for the first time to an interview on a public video recording. The speaker sounded almost identical to that of the government administrator who was charged with felony conflict of interest. I had heard that speaker was a protégé of the accused. Hearing him speak confirmed the information I had received and that led me to look again at how they were associated. Recently, I cringed when told an individual was reported saying of his enemies, "They need a dirt nap." Should I ever

hear that again, I will look carefully for an association between the parties.

9. **Visceral**—Pay attention to your physical response. If your stomach turns, your hair crawls, or you get goosebumps, it is a primal affirmation or warning to be heeded.

10. **Beware**—Beware of those in power who appoint malleable people or those who can be manipulated, follow blindly, or are incompetent. Good leaders do not need lackeys; they associate with individuals with proven ability even greater than their own.

11. **Research**—Read, watch, see, ask questions. Evaluate the associations that appear for accuracy using the methods outlined in this list. Who do your leaders glance at, lean toward in meetings, go to during breaks, socialize with, meet for lunch? Watch body language. Attend live meetings in person when possible because the video camera can't record what an acute observer sees.

12. **Power**—The real power may not lay with the person out front. Watch for who is driving the discussion and decisions. Is it the guy at the back of the room sending non-verbal signals that most people never see and that the formal meeting video recordings, focused only on the speaker, never catch? In whose car do they leave? With whom do they go out for drinks after the meeting?

13. **Insider**—Being on the inside is the best way to find out what is really going on. Just because something looks suspicious does not make it malfeasant. It is critical to verify and assess red flags, ruling them in or out because it is a waste of time and energy, inherently unfair, even paranoid, to accuse without basis. Seek first to understand.

14. **Similarities**—Do you see behaviors or situations that are like other situations in which malfeasance was involved? Follow up!

15. **Outcry**—Is there public outcry, are there whistleblowers, are you obstructed in attempts to get information that should be readily provided?

16. **Talking in Circles**—Or talking, talking, talking, talking. I have seen this ploy used in meetings in response to questions that are too incisive. The response will be so long-winded and technical that eventually the hearer is worn down and gives up, whereby the obfuscation succeeds.

17. **"It will save us so much money"**—"I am giving you such a good deal." Really? Why? This is the snag on which Board members are duped. As soon as a contractor says, "I am saving you so much money," compare apples with apples to be sure, and run the numbers to check the bottom line. The more they say it, the more you should look.

18. **Just keep saying it**—And say it in public, and it becomes Truth; what people believe no matter what comes after. Say it often enough, say it first, and it sticks as truth and is quoted as truth whether it is or not. Do not be misled by this trick. Research it yourself.

19. **Pay attention to the twinge**—Years ago, a friend who was a psychiatrist told me always to pay attention to the twinge—that little thing that makes you uncomfortable—when interviewing anyone. That will be the thing that comes back as a problem later. I have found this to be true in every case. For example, I was uncomfortable with my colleague's cavalier attitude to campaign law. She later cast her lot with others who shared her view that the fair political practice rules really weren't important.

20. **Trust your gut**—I remember being surprised when a business professor told me to trust my gut. But he was right. The left brain isn't always the right brain.

21. **Go Along to Get Along (GAGA) mentality**—If you must go along to get along, something is wrong.

PART 4

Troubleshooting

Situation + Opportunity = Trouble

CHAPTER 11 SIGNS OF THE TIMES

Wouldn't it be refreshing if instead of hearing People say, "You can't beat City Hall" we would hear City Hall saying, "You can't beat The People!"

VOCABULARY

Estate	

Before we start, let's consider the meaning of the word 'estate.' There are various dictionary definitions and explanations. 'Estate' can mean the nature and extent of an owner's rights, or it can mean any of these:

- A position of honor
- Political rights
- Ownership of assets and liabilities
- The right to enjoy assets now or later
- A state of mind
- A concept
- An idea
- A design for the future
- A planned undertaking
- A large government-supported undertaking

It is both tangible, as in assets, and intangible, as in ideas and future hopes. It derives from the word "stand," which raises the question, "For what do we stand?"

The following issues may not universally affect Town and County Halls and Councils. They are, however, significant in California, and in some cases of historical significance, so I include them as things to consider, as we look for ways we can better serve our communities.

I have enthusiastic respect for each of the City Managers I have known. They have been the professionals who understand how to run the business of the city, who must also manage large and diverse employee groups. It was City Managers who often informed and inspired me as to the potential of their communities. They have carried and inspired the vision of their Cities and driven it forward. The same goes for the employees in my City and in other government agencies with which I worked. They are dedicated, conscientious, and kind. This chapter is not a treatise on the ills of individual managers, it is a search for an evolution of roles that can grow and change in sync with technology and the welfare of communities.

Around the turn of the 20th century, as the country's population grew, the need for greater administrative assistance and professional management in its municipalities grew with it. Professional government administrators evolved to meet the need. However, as employees rather than elected representatives they are beholden to the Council majority and more recently have become too powerful. Government employees are not intended to be in post for profit motives. They are intended to be in post for service. However, in the century since these first ideas came to fruition as the population and kitty have increased, so too has the power of the local Executive branch of government.

Now they seek the income of private industry AND the security net of socialism, and in too many cases they get both. This means that huge percentages of the tax dollars meant to go to the service of The People go to provide full private-industry-level paychecks and full family health benefits for life following early retirement. Consider a small town of

45,000 like San Luis Obispo, with a Chief Executive paid upwards of $300,000 a year. The financial burden is exacerbated because public servants can retire as early as the age of fifty-five and may live to the age of ninety.

The City could be paying full salary and benefits to their retired Manager for as long as 35 years, while at the same time paying the current City Manager who will retire on full benefits and salary for 35 years. Consider that successive Managers retire after an average of five years at their highest salary. Even if the average job tenure was ten years, at any given time taxpayers could be paying full salary and benefits for up to five City Managers to do the job of one City Manager for 10 years. But it doesn't stop there because there are a hundred or more employees with similar benefits, if not as high a salary. It is reasonable for personnel costs to consume a portion of a City's budget. However, if salaries are to align with corporate remuneration, the percentage of revenue consumed by salaries should also align with corporate norms, in the thirty to forty percent range.

During my "boomer" lifetime, 'socialism' has been bandied about as a great evil. And yet, we are very much socialized. Not so much so as the more civilized European nations but more so for an elite group—government employees who reap benefits at our expense. It may not be cradle-to-grave for the employee, but it is employment-to-grave and then cradle to the employee's grave for the health care of their families. At any given time, an agency will be paying current employees full pay plus their pensions plus the PERS backlogs, PLUS all retirees until such time as they die. An agency could be supporting twice its actual number of employees—check it out! And you can be sure that it's not clearly detailed in the budget. As my son would have said as a teenager, "Mom, that's really messed up."

What is most insidious is that the same beneficiaries of this system that covers officials at full salary and benefits to the grave have direct control in the case of Congress and direct influence in the case of staff. In the case of the military, it is a fair system. It is not fair to The People if it extends to their public servants. We must find a way to use government funds for The People—the shareholders—who fund it.

As a businessperson and single parent, always reliant on my own resourcefulness to provide for my retirement, my healthcare, maternity pay, and sick pay, I admit to sour grapes that such a sizable proportion of the taxes I pay goes to providing what I never had for free whilst self-employed and never had as an elected volunteer. I willingly served 20-40 hours a week for $300 a month that didn't even cover vehicle expenses, reducing my earning power for 15 years. That is the Ben Franklin model—that citizens take time out to serve.

We need more than just our first three "estates" of government and our fourth, the press and media, now that we have grown so large. As John Adams said, we need Statesmen, Heroes, and Philosophers. You can fill this role as an elected representative with integrity, and so can our City Managers as a fifth estate.

In local government the Executive branch (City Hall) is not elected, which leads to a conflict of interest in upholding its role as one of the three estates. To redress that imbalance, it is critical that we place more emphasis on the role of the City Manager, in league with the City Attorney, as an executive estate, reframing our thinking so as to honor them as an estate, tasked as guardians of the separation of powers so critical to the citizens to whom City Hall belongs. In most Cities our Executive branch has no power to hold the Legislative or Judicial branches to account because it is appointed by and thereby beholden to the City Council majority. It is not responsive to The People as envisioned by our forefathers. It has evolved into an employer/employee relationship rather than a test of equals. If the City Manager and City Attorney were elected, they could take up the roles of the executive estate or create fifth and sixth estates.

I am a student of organizational culture. Several unhealthy government cultural trends exist that we as Councilmembers, together with professional managers dedicated to the public trust have the power to change. We need an evolution in government culture. My observations follow.

1. **Budget line items**—If it's too difficult to understand or it isn't explained, it should raise questions. Line items should reflect, rather than obscure, especially with regard to pensions, retirees, and current staff.

2. The "go along to get along" practice of **kowtowing to the Council majority** is the easy out for high level government executives, but it deprives Councils of the experience and perspective that skilled municipal staff can provide. When the City Manager and City Attorney are employed at will, the will of the Council majority, their risk is that if they do not please the Council majority, which can change with every two-year election cycle, they can find themselves out of a job. To govern well, the Council must be provided with options, straight talk, and straight facts, not just what they want to hear, and not just what agrees with their agendas.

3. On the other hand, when **staff attempt to control outcomes,** the tail begins wagging the dog. Because administrators will usually be in post long after elected officials have moved on, they learn how to game the elected officials. They do the training of the officials, thereby controlling behind the scenes and sometimes much more openly participating in deliberations. It is the elected who have been elected to make the tough decisions. Staff are there to provide the information to help them make good decisions.

4. **Aversion to controversy**—Administrators hate a brouhaha. There is a proclivity among administrators to sidle away from or gloss over anything that might cause eyebrows to raise. This is coupled with the view that the public are to be avoided when possible and the bad actions of a Council are to be kept hidden. Perhaps City Managers—the Executive — should be elected rather than appointed by the Council. And perhaps it should be the same for the City Attorney.

5. **City staff trains new government agency Board members**. The only training my colleagues and I received about

our roles was in relationship to City staff. The message was that staff run the City, and if we had questions as Councilmembers, we were to ask through the City Manager and give direction via Board majority. We also received basic Brown Act and Ethics training. The attitude was that the Brown Act was useful if the Council wished to discuss sensitive matters, but that otherwise, it was a pain in the backside because we could only talk with a minority of the Council outside meetings. In addition to training at City Hall, Councilmembers need training from independent outside sources in their roles and responsibilities as Board members.

6. This **lack of respect for the process of open meetings** was apparent statewide. The culture of City Halls was a fear of controversy and a desire to quell or avoid anything that might lead to uncomfortable exchanges. It is understandably best practice to protect the public image of an institution and its leaders. However, this has gone far awry in government agencies, and not only just with #MeToo cases. It extends to any situation with whistleblowers or Councilmember misdeeds. It is particularly heinous when it occurs to protect a racket.

When government staff who train new Councilmembers and staff who supply the reports that guide Council decisions, new Councilmembers, whether intentionally, or not are indoctrinated to think the way staff thinks. As newcomers, new Councilmembers depend on staff to introduce them to their roles and the process of governance. Being thrown in at the deep end, they adopt the prevailing culture of the organization. They can easily fall into the trap of thinking of themselves as City Hall employees and guardians of City Hall rather than guardians of The People.

Conversely, in the larger context of the County, it is easy for the County administrator to think of the elected officers who operate out of the County building and on behalf of the County, such as the Auditor, the County Clerk Recorder, and the Assessor as department heads, which they are not. They are the choice of the electorate as their representatives in these important roles of trust. They must remain independent of the bureaucracy even as they work within it.

7. **Government agencies can't/don't/won't share data.** This can be a convenient short-term way to preserve resources, as when the County Auditor says it's not his job to ride herd on agencies that report to him, and the agencies say the Auditor is supposed to keep their records. Or when the District Attorney doesn't prosecute negligence because "it's the job of the Board to exercise oversight." Or when massacres occur because reporting agencies didn't or couldn't pass on information about gun owners who may pose a risk, sometimes because computer software is incompatible. Long-term there would be financial economies of scale and reduced social suffering if government agencies used the same software or at least programs that were compatible. A culture in which agencies shift blame or do not work in tandem to problem-solve is not a healthy culture.

8. **Government agencies don't play well together.** One government agency sues another or many others, through the courts, another government agency, all on our dime. What other organization would allow its divisions to sue one another at the cost of the shareholders? And yet, we The People allow our government to continue internal spats and build fiefdoms without batting an eye, all at the expense of our best interest, stealing from ourselves by doing so. Sure, like a whispering campaign, it makes enjoyable reading, has entertainment value, and keeps the presses flowing, while everyone wins except the shareholders caught in a perpetual lose-lose cycle that they fund. The lawyers make out. The agencies ask for more money from us to cover their legal costs, therefore not impacting their operating budgets, but creating work for themselves, to the detriment of our quality of life when taxes increase to fund their spats.

Just as the ideal is that our elected representatives should be held to the highest standard, so should government agency executives and attorneys.

Where does the buck stop? If you are inclined to say, "with the City Manager," think again. The buck stops with you, the collective Council. Ideally, every member of our collective government OF The People BY The People FOR The People would take the view that the buck stops with them; that it is our role to take up our place to ensure that ours is a government that truly serves us. That, I believe, is how it was intended. Even in this scenario, you cannot shift responsibility. Far too often when I was in service, I heard Councilmembers, Mayors and candidates whine and opine, "We are just volunteers; we don't know what we are doing; we can't be held responsible if it all goes wrong." (Then, I ask, who can?) Or I heard a candidate sneer, "We are not activists," the implication being "We aren't supposed to watch out for malfeasance, we are just supposed to sit up here on the dais and pass ordinances. And hold meetings.

NOTES

 # FOR WHOM DOES THE CITY ATTORNEY WORK?

What Does the Agency Attorney Do?

First, let me explain something that even an attorney on my City Council and her followers did not seem to understand. Agency attorneys are different from County or big City District Attorneys or State or federal Attorneys General who work within the court system.

Agency attorneys sit in the meetings of the agency to advise as needed and draft the contracts and ordinances of the government agency and occasionally to act on behalf of the agency if it is sued or if the agency must sue or to line up the right experts to manage the legal matters they cannot handle themselves. Unlike the District Attorney or Attorney General, agency attorneys do not prosecute, and they do not press charges. They act more in the role of corporate attorneys, working on the day-to-day business of the agency.

Before I took up my role as the new Mayor, I was asked, "Debbie, who does the City Attorney work for?" by my friend, the constitutional attorney. Thinking back to the contracts I had seen between agency and City Attorneys, I replied, "The City of Grover Beach." Stew persisted, "Who does the City Attorney work for?" Digging deeper, I replied, "Well, he is appointed by the City Council, but he doesn't represent individual Councilmembers." Stew asked again. I was stumped. He replied, "The City Attorney works for The People. His job is to interpret the law to be sure that The People are protected. Your City is The People's institution. Our country was originally established to protect The People from their government, and the City Attorney is there to make sure that happens."

I have to agree with my friend. If you accept that the one who pays the attorney is the client, then the client in a criminal case would be an alleged criminal or a victim. The client in a corporate case would be a company. With a government agency it is The People. The People pay the attorney. The agency attorney is there to serve the interest of the ratepayers; to make sure that the work the attorney does for the agency and that the laws created serve The People and protect The People from their government.

Over the years I became increasingly aware of how often this is misunderstood and/or misrepresented or interpreted differently by agency attorneys and Boards. This is in part because insurance companies and legal firms have now inserted themselves into the business of government. They do not differentiate between the practice of corporate, criminal, and government law, even though the ownership "product" and client of each is so uniquely different that one cannot apply to the other.

This is a chicken and egg problem. It is not entirely the fault of the insurance companies or the attorneys. They would not need to work so hard to protect the agencies they should be serving on behalf of The People if The People's elected representatives behaved better. On the other hand, if they were not "covered" by insurance companies and agency attorneys, bad actors might be less prone to act badly. If The People elected representatives of the highest integrity and then exercised oversight over those they elected, their interests would be much better protected at much lower social and financial cost.

Corrupt behavior violates our good faith and our financial stability. It steals our quality of life by filching money from the things we have set up local government to provide—safe streets, utilities, sanitation, and social services. The recipients of diverted funds often become monopolies too big to fail, demanding more of our money to save ourselves further suffering from the crises they perpetrate by misusing our money, all the while continuing to retain their positions of trust and vote themselves pay raises even following criminal conviction.

In California, PG&E (Pacific Gas & Electric) failed to use profits to maintain power lines, causing wildfires that stole lives and billions of dollars as tens of thousands of their customers lost their homes.

Who pays for this? Do their shareholders? Does the Board? Does Senior Management? Do their regulators? NO. Their customers who have lost everything pay more for the services. We do—we the taxpayers who fund the courts through which legitimate lawsuits pass, we the taxpayers who fund the restoration of thousands of miles of melted phone lines, gas lines, electrical lines, sewer lines, and roads—every resident nationwide who now pays higher insurance rates to cover the losses caused by the utility's negligence.

Is this enough to make you want to demand that our institutions (monopolies) serve us rather than themselves?

On the federal level, banks were too big to fail, too big to jail, but not too big to bail. The white-collar criminals who gambled the equity of millions of people and then took their homes crashed the 2007 economy and gave themselves huge pay increases. The Federal Financial Crisis Inquiry Commission stated in a 2010 report, "Fraud, con jobs, theft, and embezzlement cost U.S. taxpayers $300-$600 billion annually—three to six times the $100 billion generated by the illegal drug trade."

In my hometown, the sewer District's reserves were in place to update old equipment with backup systems to prevent spills in the event that any part of the plant broke down. Nearly all the funds in the reserves were paid to the now-convicted executive who funneled work to his firm and then billed and rebilled to do the same work over and over.

After three whistle blowers and over a million dollars in fines, the insurance company quit insuring the agency, but the administrator didn't tell the public their sewer agency was uninsured—he just left them on the hook. The District Attorney had written indemnity into the administrator's contract. The administrator, a private contractor who should have and could have had personal errors and omissions insurance was instead covered by the agency, even as he left the agency uninsured. The Board backed him. For whom were they working? Certainly not for The People who pay their salaries and employ them to protect their health and safety.

Was a single Board member held to account for approving over-drafted budgets that took millions from the reserves and stalled a $7 million refurbishment that will now cost nine times that amount? No, but our rates are now ten times higher than they were at the time the corruption started because we still need the back-up systems and had to pay the $1.3 million fine levied not against the Board or the convicted executive, but against the sewer District customers when the system actually did fail.

Members of the public are frustrated. Somehow the guilty—and their attorneys—do not appear to "get" that what they are doing is a violation of the public trust or is wrong. They continue to operate as they have always operated, (because they CAN) even as they go to court—plea bargaining to get away with things, defending themselves using public money in the case of corrupt agencies to fund buy offs and legal fees. Those around them are complicit when they turn a blind eye or refuse to believe what is right there in front of them.

Wouldn't it be less expensive for us to pay attention and demand that those who serve us do so efficiently and with integrity, that they simply do their jobs and tell us the truth?

GOVERNMENT CANNOT DECIDE WHAT IS GOOD FOR US TO KNOW, AND WHAT IS GOOD FOR US NOT TO KNOW

Elected representation with integrity is difficult. Decision-making in the public arena—conversations, negotiations, consensus is hard for almost everyone. It is unnerving to be open and forthright on camera where every gaff shows. It is also difficult for staff who hate controversy and must kowtow to the Board majority to keep their jobs. It is much easier to leave the public out than to draw them in. It is painful to have to perform in the limelight where all your mistakes, bloopers, failures to understand are streaming live and recorded; where critics wait for the opportunity to tear you apart and smear your name for years to come. It is easier to avoid the accountability, even embarrassment, that comes from exposing our questions and views in front of not only cameras but the audience of the local people whose expectation is that we will represent them. Even for the sincere, it is less painful to go along with those who actively seek secrecy.

In private companies, silence clauses to protect company secrets are wise. Not so in government. In private companies, attorneys represent senior executives and the company against legal action. In The People's business it is The People's interest that the attorney must protect, rather than covering for the slip-ups of City Hall or elected officials. Government agencies should never use silence clauses to protect the agency or to protect government officials who misbehave, except in legitimate cases of security or human relations. Payouts by insurance companies to employees for misconduct of government officials should be public information, and the offender should pay if convicted.

The People do not give their public servants the right to decide what is good for The People to know and what is not good for them to know. (Sunshine Law) And yet, repeatedly I have seen agency attorneys doing just that—deciding what is good for The People to know and what is not good for them to know. When this happens, The People are denied control over the government they have created—or elected. If the City Attorney thinks it is his job to cover for errant officials, elected or employed, who harass staff, or who are terminated for raiding the cookie jar, then The People are NOT protected. Their money is simply used to cover payouts, and then they keep reelecting or reappointing the same corrupt people who realize they can get away with it.

JUSTICE DELAYED IS JUSTICE DENIED

Rabbi Mayerberg's 1929 *KC Star* opinion piece expressed it well, "… crime can be held in check, not by severity of the penalty, but by the speed and certainty with which justice is rendered. Let … the legal procedure be rid of all the technicalities by which testimony is hidden or perverted or delays are manufactured; in brief, establish a swiftly moving machinery of justice in America."

There should be no statute of limitation for crimes against The People by their government. That takes away at least some of the incentive to stall. It is unethical to use The People's money to delay with arduous information requests, to bankrupt a whistleblower in order to block a lawsuit. The People deserve quick efficacious solutions. Failures of the public trust should be addressed immediately. No errant public servant should ever be aided by a public agency attorney.

Delivering efficient and speedy justice is one of the fundamental duties of any government. If the government fails to do so, it fails in its duty to protect its citizens against further criminal activities. It also fails to issue a warning to potential criminals, thereby becoming less capable of checking unlawful activities.

When the judicial system takes too long to investigate a case and mete out proper justice, evidence gets less and less reliable. Documents are lost, witnesses die, and prosecuting parties run out of money. There is also more scope for tampering with or losing evidence, further stress, and threat of harm to witnesses and prosecutors.

Time and again in my own County, government agencies would stall and stall until statutes of limitation ran out, proving the proverb that justice delayed is justice denied. As time passes people forget or leave town. Taking away the statute of limitation for crimes by government would ensure that public agencies cannot deny justice by delaying.

What could the County District Attorney do? In most Counties grand juries do not have subpoena power, only oversight. However, the County District Attorney or the State Attorney General has the power to call a criminal Grand Jury, but if they don't do so or don't prosecute, the job of taking apart corruption is left to federal Grand Juries.

Shortly after I was elected as the first directly elected female Mayor in my town, a former City Attorney came up to congratulate me at a community pancake breakfast. An unassuming character, his generosity and vision always eclipsed his means. #MeToo hadn't surfaced yet, so I wasn't expecting what he said next. Perhaps he had been following the news or was aware of my approach to governance, or it was because I am a woman, but he assumed that I had heard historic accounts of young women being assaulted by members of the City Council, as indeed I had. "You know, there were some things I didn't do right. Those girls were right. They deserved to be protected, and instead, I protected the Councilmember who should have been in jail." It happened in the sixties and seventies, and history repeated itself in 2008.

Later, as the "#Me Too" movement was beginning, my membership in the California League of Cities Women's Caucus gave me an opening to speak on the issue of public agencies funding and hiding the defense of senior staff or politician sexual harassment of employees or community members. The Women's Caucus asked each of us to request that our Councils publicly take a stand against this behavior. I raised the issue in a Council meeting during Council committee comments.

A female Council colleague with a law degree reported out to members of the public that I was going to get the council sued. She was thinking like a lawyer, not like a representative of The People, making the same mistake made by agency lawyers—the person who would get the agency sued is the perpetrator, not the person who calls for justice. If the representatives behave themselves, neither they nor their victims nor the whistle blowers are likely to get their agency sued!

To sue in a case such as this is the very essence of our democracy; the very reason for our courts—to ensure justice; to give the minority a voice. Furthermore, the victim SHOULD sue the agency if the agency is in collusion with the perpetrator. The perpetrator should pay the agency costs, and the perpetrator should pay the victim damages. The institution put in place to SERVE the public is not there to serve the interests of the elected or their appointed, nor is it there to hide the crimes they commit and cover under color of authority.

I don't know the details of the three Grover Beach employees allegedly sexually harassed by elected officials. I do know that soon after they reported being sexually harassed, they no longer worked for the City, while the Mayor kept his post and was re-elected for another 10 years. The City swears everyone to silence because it is a human relations matter. One whistleblower was told it would be best if she just left town, and she did.

Corporate lawyers can legitimately buy silence. Corporations deal in trade secrets and information that could hurt their ability to remain competitive, or even stay in business, if released. The government does not have trade secrets to protect. Government is a monopoly with guaranteed recurring income. Transparency will not put it out of business. The Brown Act is unambiguous: government may not decide what is good for us to know and what is not good for us to know.

Government agency lawyers too often practice law, not of The People and for The People, to protect The PEOPLE from bad government as initially intended, but to hide crimes committed under the color (power) of office, while in office, and often, even before taking office. Agency attorneys wrongly often see themselves as the City Attorney, or the Council Attorney, or the "hush it up guy" who makes sure no one at the City is ever embarrassed, rather than the attorney who protects The People from their government. Government agencies and their attorneys have applied the silence clause of "trade secrets" to cover human relations travesties, to gag and buy off the victims of staff or elected officials in cases of sexual harassment, racism, and whistleblowing.

Things have changed; mostly because of the "#MeToo" movement, but they haven't changed enough. The movement has promulgated laws and lawsuits to protect victims of sexual crimes, but these protections do not go far enough. The Racketeering Influenced Corrupt Organizations Act was created as a means of taking down Mafia organizations, and it now also addresses government corruption, but it doesn't fully protect The People because while it incentivizes and makes it possible for The People to sue their government, the payout comes from taxpayer funds.

Corporate legal practice has also migrated to government agencies in a way that serves the bureaucracy rather than The People the bureaucracy serves. I see two other problems with agency attorneys. Just as in criminal law, if elected representatives make a mistake that could result in prosecution, agency attorneys counsel them to deny everything; never admit guilt and buy silence. In institutions predicated on transparency, they threaten the victims that if they are paid off in what may be legitimate damages, they may never speak about their experience, as if bullying and harassment were trade secrets to be protected. These aren't competitive advantages that threaten the survival of the shareholders if divulged. These are practices that threaten the shareholders if NOT divulged.

These cover-ups run counter to open government. The cover up is possible because there is a loophole in the Brown Act that our representatives often seek to apply too liberally. Lawsuits, potential lawsuits, and employee matters may be discussed in closed session hearings. The other obstacle to transparency is "attorney privilege," which gives politicians and lawyers the cover of secrecy and gives other parties to the communication the requirement of confidentiality.

This approach is a violation of the oath we take to protect The People we serve from attacks within and without. When a representative of The People attacks or assaults one of The People or misuses authority or position that is an attack from within that we are sworn to root out. Hush money payouts are hidden to the public if they are covered by insurance. They are "off budget items." If not, they are hidden by being thrown in with related budget items where they won't show, such as salaries or employee benefits. Payouts should be a separate line item and if the insurance company won't cover it, further investigation is needed to find out why.

Government, like the Catholic church, has covered up leaders' transgressions and bought off those transgressed against to avoid bad publicity, leaving a trail of destruction along the way, but in the case of government, it affects the entire population, not just the membership of one organization. At least in the church, parishioners can stop giving. If we are unhappy with government, we cannot stop paying our taxes. Joint Powers Insurance Authorities formed by government agencies do not act for The People whose tax dollars fund their agencies. While on the payroll of the public purse they act for corrupt, negligent, and incompetent government officials.

The good news of late is that new laws no longer allow government agencies to hide the sexual misconduct of their elected officials. States are banning nondisclosure agreements that cover sexual harassment. In September 2018, California banned the agreements in cases involving sexual assault, harassment, or sex discrimination. New York and New Jersey enacted similar laws. New York went further, expanding its sexual harassment law to cover independent contractors in 2018 and improved protections for domestic workers in 2019. California went as far as to protect certain working relationships, including those with film producers.

Congress reformed its process for staffers reporting sexual harassment. Allegations against legislators on both sides of the aisle have drawn attention to the issue of sexual misconduct by members of Congress, and Congress has taken steps to reform itself as a workplace.

It can be justified to have employee matters heard confidentially. Is it justified to keep the bad actor's behavior silent? In one case recently following similar behavior on the part of our former Mayor, the County of Santa Barbara said not. The #MeToo movement has forced government attorneys and harassers out into the open. Now there are experts who determine whether such claims are credible, and finally accusations against our former mayor were determined to be credible, and after ogling and making lewd comments about a staffer and customer of the agency, he had to resign from his government job.

There remain gaps in these laws. Honoring fully the value of open government, these protections need to apply equally to any kind of harassment, racism, and whistle blowing, exposing and punishing the perpetrators rather than doling out large sums of taxpayer funds or campaign donations to avoid embarrassment, protect officeholders, and silence victims. Whistleblowers are still subject to silence clauses.

Those suffering harassment not of a sexual nature are not yet covered by law. Our County cabal's hired gun fulfilled his job of firing our sewer plant's whistle-blowing superintendent at a cost of over $200,000 to the agency. The hired gun was more richly rewarded, retiring at the age of fifty on full salary with full health care for his family of four for life, at a far, far higher cost to the ratepayers of the sewer District.

Several times I have seen a situation in which a government employee becomes a whistleblower or is harassed sexually or otherwise by a Councilmember, Mayor, or senior staff member. This automatically gets shut behind closed doors for one of two reasons: it becomes the threat of possible legal action, and it is a personnel matter. The victim is stuck behind closed doors, outnumbered by lawyers and staff and scared to make it public when the same lawyers and staff and Councilmembers are threatening to expose real or made-up failings and threatening future employment or dangling the carrot of a large payout and no public embarrassment if the victim agrees to a silence clause, all using government funds or insurance money that leads to higher insurance costs or even refusal by insurers to insure as was the case at our sewer plant.

The next question that arises is, who pays the silence money to the employee? Should it be The People? There's an argument that if we elect bad people who hire bad people, then yes, we pay. However, it is usually paid on the quiet by insurance companies or buried in the budget and not disclosed or itemized. The next step is that all who were bound by government silence clauses in cases of harassment of any kind should be declared free of those clauses. Looking at it in these terms, it begins to look like trafficking: a member of staff is harassed. They are paid off and bound. And we pay for that?

Shouldn't government attorneys be looking after the best interests of the citizens rather than finding ways to cover for corrupt officials?

Shouldn't the insurance agencies to whom we then have to pay higher insurance fees or higher deductibles be looking after the best interests of the public who pays their premiums rather than agreeing to huge silence clauses and payouts?

Silence clauses should not apply to the operations of local government. If agency funds are impacted either by higher premiums or payouts, then the public has a right to know. The decision about privacy should be that of the victim, not of the perpetrator. Taking it one step further, the perpetrator should pay.

And is it really appropriate that our tax dollars or campaign donations are paid in good faith and then used to cover up bad faith activities? I have had whistle blowers beg me to find a way to subpoena them because that is the only way they can talk.

For many years I believed, as many elected and appointed representatives also seem to believe, that we could rely on agency attorneys to keep us on the right side of the law, and out of court. I did not research, confirm, or verify any of the information provided by our attorneys or by staff. The only alternate opinions I heard came from members of the public responding to agency actions or proposed actions that they questioned or opposed.

While Councilmembers should be able to rely on staff and agency attorneys, we mustn't become too comfortable doing so.

When you consider any issue where the question of law or interpretation or a dispute arises, always go back to the law, and read it and read cases that follow it. If it is incredibly complex, find an attorney who cares about constitutional law or local government and ask them to interpret it for you. Sometimes that will be the City Attorney, but if you sense you're not getting the whole answer or the attorney is hedging, go outside City Hall for answers. Sometimes you can even find answers by googling.

HONEST FIXES

The role of agency attorneys should be a neutral role at the very minimum, advising on the law surrounding charges brought by employees, which should be investigated by an outside third party rather than the attorney.

While large payouts may 'compensate' the victims for their suffering, compensation should compensate, not censor, censure, suppress, or silence to keep the truth concealed and sanitize public records. When agencies swear staff to silence and swear the victims to silence, the perpetrators go free to offend again. In the matter of hiding corruption and buying silence, the government and corporate practice must reach a critical fork in the road.

Just as we need to teach best Boardsmanship practice for elected officials, we need to raise up lawyers who champion good governance and recognize that business and criminal law practices cannot be applied across the Board to government agencies. The People's money belongs to The People, not to the lawyers who profit by protecting self-serving representatives.

MITIGATE DON'T LITIGATE

The government has deep pockets into which income keeps flowing. They are a perpetual piggy bank fed by taxes. The ability to increase income by pursuing legal action is a very real conflict of interest for agency lawyers. Inasmuch as it is a conflict for agency lawyers, it is a conflict for politicians. They know that there will always be more money flowing in. Taxpayer funds are the fountain that never runs dry. There is no incentive to be as careful or as accountable as they would be if it were finite or dependent on their performance. As for agency attorneys, the more they can play on the egos or inexperience of the politicians to get them involved in lawsuits, the more money they earn. Just as a good politician acts not in his or her own interests but in the interests of those governed, a good lawyer keeps his clients out of court. While this conflict is regulated by private clients' reluctance to overspend, it is much less carefully monitored by members of the public, their institutions, and elected officials.

The courts are the legitimate resource for solving disputes that cannot otherwise be determined. They are the wrong place for suits between government agencies. Where government agencies are at odds, let the government, that is, the legislators figure it out without taking up court time and wasting tax dollars to fund one government agency against another using a third publicly funded system, the courts. When public agencies use the legal system to do battle with one another, the taxpayers pay three times. As my parents said when they divorced, "Only the lawyers got rich."

Agency attorneys are in the same tenuous position as staff and government contractors, there at the whim of the ruling body, so it is risky not to go along to get along. It would be more appropriate if their tenure were at the whim of the voters, and they were able to act independently of the agency if necessary. This is a compelling argument for electing agency attorneys rather than having them appointed by a Board majority. The counterargument by staff and Councils will be that it is expensive to add another position to the ballot. Indeed, it is, but much less expensive than hiring attorneys who are working for the Council majority rather than The People who elect them. It is much less expensive than the money spent on unnecessary citizen-funded lawsuits and hush money payouts.

Another protection against government attorney conflicts of interest would be to mandate that outside counsel be used for government agency lawsuits. This is often the case, but not always, and a mandate would temper the temptation to bolster personal income by agitating agencies into lawsuits.

THE EXCEPTION—A "NO TOLERANCE" RULE

There are times when government must prosecute to protect The People. When someone defrauds The People, failing to prosecute the offender rewards his behavior and sends him off to steal again, costing far more in the long term than prosecuting immediately. Any crime against The People should be immediately prosecuted both as a deterrent to the offender and to other would-be offenders and a protection for The People.

If the City Manager and City Attorney were elected posts, the following chart of the three estates would look much more like the chart at the national level, the one that the framers of our Constitution intended to safeguard us.

We, the People
TWO BRANCHES OF LOCAL GOVERNMENT
State Constitution
(provides no separation
of powers)
Local Government if Executive Branch were Elected.
JUDICIAL
(interprets laws)
State
Court
Other
Federal
Courts
LEGISLATIVE
(makes laws)
City Council and Mayor
EXECUTIVE (carries out laws)
City Manager
City
Attorney
Police
Chief
Department
Heads

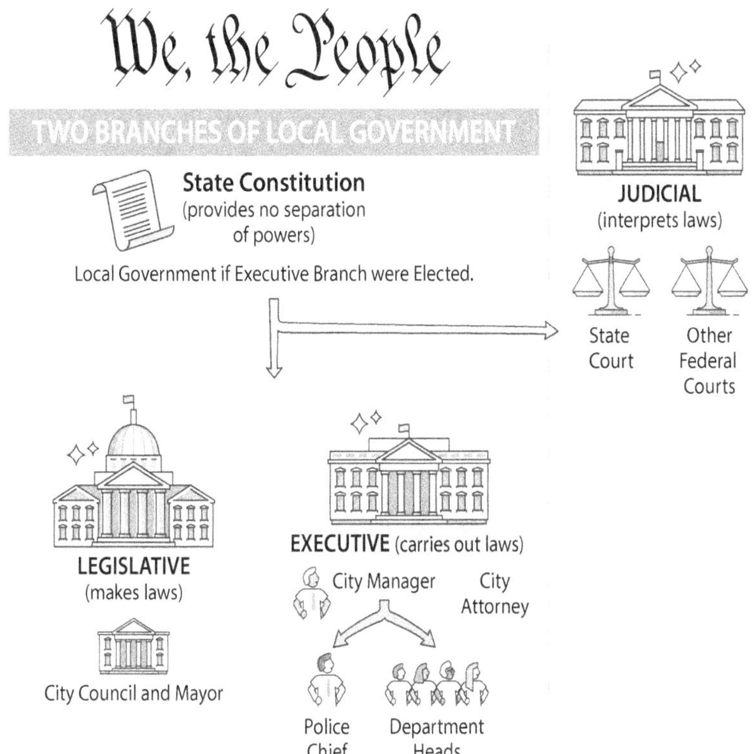

NOTES

The Seventh Estate. We The People. Never forget why you are in office. You are there to serve. If you practice good Boardsmanship, oversight, and open government, making sure always to give The People a voice, you will have come a long way in ensuring good governance in our government of The People, by The People, and for The People.

- By now you know your roles and responsibilities on various government Boards.

- You know what questions to ask in order to exercise responsible oversight.

- You recognize patterns of behavior that can function as a warning that questions must be asked.

- You are equipped to participate in a local government meeting, and you understand the order of the meeting.

- You understand why meetings are run the way they are run, and you have the context to engage effectively.

- You understand the history of local government and why it seems different from State or national government.

- You know why government is run so differently from a non-profit organization or a business corporation.

- You understand the ups and downs, and the positives and negatives of a government by, of, and for The People that relies on the common man and woman to take up their part in the system.

+ You know how to exercise oversight effectively.

+ You are a public servant.

If you listen, engage your community, and treat all with respect you will serve with integrity. It is my prayer that you will be a member of a Board that serves well and that you continue that cycle of integrity. If it's otherwise, check out the Appendices for more information.

When you need more help or inspiration go to https://DebbiePeterson.com for links to:

+ Contact me.

+ Read or Comment on my Blog

+ Listen to my podcast *Corruption Chronicles*

+ Read *The HAPPIEST CORRUPTION: Sleaze, Lies, & Suicide in a California Beach Town*

+ Take my online course, *Double Dais—Adventures in Local Government*

+ Book me for a speaking engagement

+ Have a one-on-one session or consultation with me

+ Have a group session. I can tailor-make programs:
  □ For a conference, seminar, workshop
  □ For your governing body
  □ For your staff

+ Sign up to be notified of events and publication dates

Consultations and speaking engagements are available in person or via online platforms.

 # THE UNASSAILABLE PUBLIC RECORDS REQUEST

For more information go to my podcast, *Corruption Chronicles* to learn from the author of this Request and go to my online course, *Double Dais—Adventures in Local Government*. Hopefully as a Councilmember you will not have to resort to a formalized request for information. However, this may be the only way you can get the information, or you may be approached by citizens struggling to get information from a government agency.

Any time you would like information from local government, you are entitled to it, within reason, and provided there is no legal exclusion to releasing the information. In California such a request is often referred to as a PRA which stands for the Public Records Act. The press and media often refer to it by the federal version, FOIA—the Freedom Of Information Act. A word of caution—anything submitted to a government agency becomes public record and is also subject to public records requests. If you submit a FOIA request online, the request will be retained online and available to the public. According to the Brown Act you can even ask local agencies in California to mail out agendas to you, although they can ask you to provide postage. You can also be asked to provide DVDs or Thumb Drives and/or pay for photocopying, but only the actual cost of the media, excluding staff time to prepare the information.

For this reason, delivery via email is preferable because there is then a digital record, and the agency cannot charge for it. If you need information, search first on the agency's website. If it isn't there, you can simply go to City Hall, email them, or call, and ask for it.

Sometimes they will tell you your request must be made in writing. Not so. They cannot legally make that demand. However, it is best practice to have a record of requests both for understanding the request itself, and for the record. If it is at all complicated or lengthy it's best to make a written request. Why? Because written requests themselves are public record, as is the response of the agency to your request. The more difficult it is to get an answer, the more thorough your request should be.

Don't let an obstructive or uninformed staffer thwart your request. The agency is required to provide the information within 10 days or provide a response within 10 days as to why it cannot respond in that time frame with an estimate of when it will provide the information.

The public records request template that follows is based on California law. Often it is not necessary to quote the letter of the law to public agencies, but if you are getting the run-around, it may well elicit what you need. Any attempt to avoid providing information should be considered a red flag and investigated further.

Similar laws exist in other States. In some cases, you may not need or wish to include the amount of detail in the template included here. Be sure to provide as much detail as possible for every piece of information you seek. If the agency does not comply, take it to your County District Attorney (DA), and ask the DA to enforce it.

An internet search may also turn up guidance in your particular location. I call this template the unassailable public records request because the constitutional attorney I consult suggests that this is the best one to use, even better than many he sees from attorneys.

[Ref. # starting with year, then month, then day, i.e., 20221218-CPRA]

[YOUR NAME]
[YOUR STREET ADDRESS]
[YOUR CITY, STATE ZIPCODE]
[YOUR PHONE AND TEXT NUMBER OR NUMBERS]
[YOUR EMAIL ADDRESS]
[DAY OF THE WEEK, DATE]

[AGENCY HEAD OR CLERK]
[AGENCY NAME]
[AGENCY STREET ADDRESS]
[AGENCY CITY, STATE ZIPCODE]
[AGENCY PHONE NO.]
[AGENCY EMAIL ADDRESS]

VIA: [List how it was sent/delivered: E-MAIL AND/OR U.S. MAIL CERTIFIED DELIVERY AND/OR FAX AND/OR HAND DELIVERY]
SUBJECT: CALIFORNIA PUBLIC RECORDS ACT REQUEST
[Ref #: (from the top of this page)]

Dear [contact name],

Pursuant to the California Public Records Act ("CPRA") (Gov. Code §6250 et seq.1), this is a request for disclosure of public records from your office. A response to this request is required by law within ten days. (§6253, subd. (c).)

The Legislature "finds and declares that access to information concerning the conduct of the people's business is a fundamental and necessary right of every person in this state." (Ibid.)

The California Constitution declares: "The people have the right of access to information concerning the conduct of the people's business, and, therefore, the meetings of public bodies and the writings of public officials and agencies shall be open to public scrutiny." (CA Const, Art I, Sect 3, subd (b).)

Before deciding that a record is exempt from disclosure, an agency should consider that "[a] statute, court rule, or other authority … shall be broadly construed if it furthers the people's right of access, and narrowly construed if it limits the right of access." (CA Const, Art I, Sect 3, subd (b), Para (2).)

The following records are requested:

1. All writings pertaining to [enter what it is you are looking for] or any other proximal matter in regards or relating to the [the name of the agency] [from the start date you are seeking information to the end date].

2. Disclosure is requested to include, but not be limited to, writings pertaining to any of the following:

   - [Start the list of what you want and list until complete.]

3. [When your list is complete make this the final item in the list.] Any communication or writing involving any person, public or private, involving the above or any proximal matter (to include writings involving any [Agency Name] or [Agency Name] staff, consultant, supplier, contractor, or legislative Board member).

The purpose of this request is to obtain information pertaining to the public interest and the people's business as conducted by the [AGENCY NAME] Board, Contractors, Service Providers, Legal Advisors, Staff and Employees. The necessity of this request is to obtain documents and correspondence related to [write a very brief description of the request], and the meetings and writings of public officials and agencies.

You are encouraged to contact me regarding scope of this request if you have any questions.

Where disclosable records are held in an electronic format by your agency, disclosure is requested to be in its ORIGINAL electronic format. (Gov. Code §6253.9.) Electronic disclosure is requested to be transmitted via electronic mail. Where electronic mail is not possible (e.g., in the case of large files), delivery may be affected via optical disc, common Internet protocols (e.g., HTTP, FTP, etc.) or by other stipulated arrangement. I am pleased to provide blank media upon request. If you are unable to deliver via e-mail please contact me at the text, telephone or email numbers noted above and I will arrange to pick up the information.

An agency may not delay or obstruct the inspection or copying of public records. Purposeful delay—even within the statutory maximum time limits—violates the CPRA. Notification of denial of any request for records shall set forth the names and titles or positions of each person responsible for the denial. (Gov. Code §6253(d).)

In the event any portion of the above request does not effectively describe an identifiable record, your agency is required to "assist the member of the public to identify records and information that are responsive to the request or to the purpose of the request" and to "provide suggestions for overcoming any practical basis for denying access to the records or information sought." (Gov. Code §6253.1.)

<u>A public agency is required to make a reasonable effort to elicit additional clarifying information from the requestor.</u> (Id., §6253.1(b).)

[Repeat the reference number and subject matter at the top of each page 20221218-CPRA]

 # HOW DO CRIMINALS OPERATE?

- The higher-ups distance themselves from physical intimidation tactics, using lackeys to do their dirty work, making requests in coded language. Like the Wizard of Oz, they operate from behind an opaque curtain, pulling the levers of a machine, with a body of minions doing their bidding, which has no place in governance and every place in criminal practice.

- Set up multiple shell companies under different names and ownership.

- Use cash for transactions, rather than leave a paper trail. This is why legalizing cannabis business while forcing cannabis companies to trade in cash because they cannot use the banking system perpetuates money laundering and perpetuates the lack of accountability that pervades cash transactions.

- Culture of fear of reprisals or public embarrassment to silence any who might speak ill of them.

- Threats to businesspeople concerning their workplaces or future tax investigations or refusal of permits or fines.

- Addiction is common.

- No tolerance for diversity of thought as voiced by Fidel Castro, "All criticism is opposition. All opposition is counter revolutionary."

- Control the estates of government. They get a stronghold in the court system, placing people in positions of power, in the planning and building departments, as fire chiefs, in the police department. They control the political bodies, thereby controlling the administrative (executive) side of government.

+ Control the message, by turning the tables, using the press, and often managing to make the criminal become the victim and the righteous or the whistleblowers become the bad guys, painted as crazy or as persecutors. They figure out what their accusers will say of them and quickly accuse their opponents of the very crimes they have committed before their opponents can point the finger at them.

+ Never let up so that their opponents are caught up in endless drama and nonsense, taking away their ability to use their executive brains, leaving them in constant fight or flight mode.

+ Whistleblower is painted as the bad guy and positioned as the "outsider" or "not one of us."

+ Dismiss opponents' claims as "sour grapes" arising out a political rivalry. Opposition is framed as political rivalry.

+ Demonize and label opponents, dehumanizing them, making it easier and easier until it becomes acceptable to attack or hate them.

+ Public works, even if not completed, are always the promise of something good to come.

+ Control assignment of lucrative government contracts, and then move on to own or control companies that get the contracts.

 # WHITE COLLAR (GOVERNMENT) CRIMINAL TRAITS

RESOURCES

- https://www.learning-mind.com/dark-triad-traits/

- https://www.embroker.com/blog/
white-collar-crime-statistics/

- Psychology/Forensic Psychology—https://exploringyour
mind.com/the-white-collar-criminal-characteristics-and-psy-
chological-traits/

In his 2002 white paper on combatting government vendor fraud, Carl Knudson, the IRS investigator who brought down Oliver North and the Colombian drug cartels, detailed the Association of Certified Fraud Examiners' profile data on fraud schemes. He advised staying on top of the latest research. I have underlined 2022 data. Knudson wrote that fraud is most likely perpetrated by someone who is:

- **30+ years or older**—The average white-collar criminal is 41 years old—University of Cincinnati School of Criminal Justice.

- **Male**—75%. A gender breakdown of defendants in financial scandals from 2001—2018 found that just 7% of those involved were women.

- **Has a stable family situation that adds to the mystique of invulnerability**—Over half (62%) of white-collar criminals are married, and 50% own homes.—University of Cincinnati School of Criminal Justice.

- **Has above-average education—white-collar, not blue-collar.** About half of occupational fraud perpetrators have a university degree.—2020 Global Study on Occupational Fraud and Abuse.

- **Less likely to have a criminal record**

- **Appears to be in good psychological health**

- **Has attained a position of trust and approachability**—Has a good reputation.

- **Knows accounting and reporting systems and their weaknesses**—Allowing him to cover a paper trail.

- **Is successful and refined**

In my County, this was illustrated on three fairly recent occasions. A Chamber of Commerce Businessperson of the year was appointed, while all along he was operating a real estate title deed scheme that, according to the Department of Justice, robbed 1,200 County residents in a $100 million fraud. Another Chamber of Commerce Man of the Year was jailed soon after for sex acts on minors. Rotarians knew both gentlemen well, just as they did the man who was convicted of double dealing in his position as the sewer District administrator and engineer. Soon after his arrest, the American Association of Engineers presented him with an award.

Knudson, referenced above, identified ways to guard against government fraud. He suggested:

- Social media and news searches to uncover hits on publicized criminal activity and civil litigation

- Searching historical data on business entities or individuals, to detect business fronts that pose for companies with conflicts of interest between company executives and government agencies, cross-checking addresses, and business locations

+ Searching public records databases

+ Subscribing to paid searches that can provide further information

+ (2022) Google all information for links and relationships

In 2022 psychologists are indicating that the profile most closely associated with those who commit white collar crimes is that of the psychopath or sociopath. While it is an alarming profile (and should be, given the widespread harm they do) these characteristics closely fit the white-collar criminals I came across in my time working with local government.

Because they are complex and psychologists are still trying to understand them, psychopaths and sociopaths make for good television drama and devastating political outcomes. They are dangerous, sometimes physically, certainly financially when they are white-collar.

SOCIOPATH/PSYCHOPATH CHARACTERISTICS

Sociopaths and psychopaths differ. The following are traits associated with both, with the exception that psychopaths are calculating, whereas sociopaths are impulsive:

+ Impulsive and hot-headed

+ Stressed when under pressure

+ Cannot maintain a normal working life

+ Can have relationships, but they find them difficult to maintain

+ Prone to over-the-top outbursts and rage

+ Sociopaths know what they do is wrong but rationalize their behavior

+ Understand other people's distress but do not care

+ Manipulative and charming.

+ Sulk and ignore people if things don't go their way

+ Low tolerance for criticism

+ Put others down

+ No qualms about manipulating others for their own gain

+ Explosive and controlling

+ Take lying to unthinkable extremes

Note that having some of these qualities does not make a person a psychopath. Psychopaths are criminals. Not all people with psychopathic qualities are criminals.

Do background checks on all white-collar positions. Insist that the HR department use The Dirty Dozen Scale, created by psychology professors Dr. Peter Jonason and Gregory Webster to measure for narcissistic, Machiavellian, and psychopathic traits. You do not have to be a psychologist to spot these traits and weed them out of government service.

In relationship to others, they are:

+ Flatterers

+ Unconcerned about the morality of their actions

+ Mean and insensitive

+ Cynical

+ Need the admiration of others

+ Crave attention

+ Want favors from others

+ Seek status and prestige

Psychopaths and sociopaths cannot perform as civil servants. They not only do not serve us; they are incapable of serving us. If hired, check the ethics of those who hired them. Do not elect them. Michelle Liew, a staff writer at Learning Mind compiled the above lists and offers the following advice:

> "Stay away from them. Do not do business with them, do not hire them—recognize the signs. If they are in leadership or official positions, avoid contact whenever possible. Use emails if you need to contact them."

Summing up or "mathing" white collar corruption, Knudson says the formula is:

$$SITUATION + OPPORTUNITY = TROUBLE$$

WHITE COLLAR/BLACK HAT

Often there is a crossover between white collar crime and more notorious in-your-face crime. The political machines of the late 1800s and early 1900s had Mafia links. My City Council awarded cannabis dispensary permits only to felons.

WHO COMMITS WHITE-COLLAR CRIME?

EM Broker quotes the following research:

- 2022: University of Cincinnati School of Criminal Justice found that 94% of white-collar crime perpetrators are the only criminals in their family, and most have spent 1-5 years with their employer.

PWC, 2020 Global Economic Crime and Fraud Survey found:

- 37% of white-collar crimes were committed by an internal perpetrator.

- 20% of crimes committed by internal perpetrators resulted from collusion with outsiders.

- 34% were committed by middle management.

- 31% were committed by operations staff.

- 26% were committed by senior management.

- Frauds committed by people who were invited in—such as employees, executives, vendors, supplier, partners, etc.—represent half of all frauds reported.

It's difficult to understand the reaction of much of society to this kind of crime. That is, until you look at what psychologists now have to say about the profile of white-collar criminals. This may help explain why people tend to euphemize it, make excuses for it, and explain it away and why it attracts such favorable treatment in the courts and prisons.

2022 PROFILING THE WHITE-COLLAR CRIMINAL

Psychopaths and sociopaths: people who lie, cheat, and swindle others for their own benefit or simply for fun or pleasure.

- Psychopaths see people like pieces on a chessboard. They are able to move them as and when they like to achieve their own aims.

- They are unable to differentiate right from wrong. They simply don't understand why cheating or lying is reprehensible.

- They "empathize" in order to camouflage themselves within society and thus go unnoticed.

- They not only set their own rules, but they also try to control the lives of others.

- In most cases, they appear as charming people, even charismatic.

- They pretend that they live perfectly normal lives. For this reason, many experts consider these criminals to be the most dangerous.

Their behavior:

- Callous and hostile, interpreting others' behavior as hostile

- Determined to get revenge

- Impulsive

- Relationship problems

- Cunning and scheming

- Little concern for the safety of others or for themselves

- Excessive alcohol consumption, drug abuse, compulsive gambling, unsafe sex, and dangerous hobbies, including criminal activities

 # WHAT EXACTLY IS CORRUPTION?

Without a legal background, as I began to encounter corruption, I found it difficult to describe the patterns of behavior I was uncovering. I observed, listened carefully, and researched meticulously to name and stop the outflow of public funds to certain contractors and elected officials, who were protected by staff and Councilmembers fearing for their jobs, and unchallenged by business owners afraid for their businesses and reputations, all frightened for their families. Now I have the words:

- **Bribery**—Offering, promising, giving, accepting, or asking for something of value to prompt an illegal or unethical action, or a breach of trust. Also referred to as Payola. Example: County Supervisor is paid by Cannabis Mogul for favorable decisions by the Board of Supervisors.

- **Coercion**—Exploiting a position of authority to pressure another to do something which he or she would not otherwise do, abuse of a relationship, the threat of taking away from another something he possesses. Example: Employees must do as a County Supervisor wishes or lose their jobs.

- **Collusion** –An agreement between parties to commit actions to deceive or defraud. Example: Agency officials covering up for staff members who steal public funds or sexually harass staff rather than reporting them to law enforcement.

- **Dark Money**—Donating money in the name of a company, ally, or employee, or through a PAC not identifiable as the source in order to hide the source. A form of money laundering—it is sneaky, but it looks innocuous. Example: Multiple campaign donations from applicants to Councilmembers for City permits under the name of an organization not on the application. It is now illegal under California law to give more than $250 if an application is underway.

- **Embezzlement**—Dishonest and illegal appropriation, use, or trafficking of the public funds, goods, or office by an officeholder for personal enrichment. Example: paying for a home kitchen remodel with a public agency's credit card.

- **Extortion**—Using coercive threats, directly or indirectly, under color of authority to demand unmerited cooperation or compensation. Example: Demand by a County Supervisor that a businessperson cease advertising in a newspaper if the businessperson wants favorable planning decisions.

- **Fraud**—Deceiving someone to gain an unfair or illegal advantage: financial, political, or otherwise. Example: Hiding last minute donations in order to win an election.

- **Malfeasance**—An act by a public official that is legally unjustified, harmful, or contrary to law, wrongdoing. Example: an agency official hiring his own firm to do work for the agency.

- **Misfeasance**—Performance of an official duty in an improper or unlawful manner or with an improper or corrupt motive. Example: Sexual harassment of members of staff.

- **Money Laundering**—Moving illicitly obtained money through multiple entities to conceal its identity, source, and destination. Example: using a chain of Limited Liability Companies (LLC) to hide payouts to public officials.

- **Nonfeasance**—Failure to act when under an obligation to do so; a refusal (without sufficient excuse) to do that which it is your legal duty to do. Example: Upon finding that a vote will not go their way, the day before a vote, six directors and their alternates announce they cannot attend a Board meeting, thus causing a cancellation of the meeting.

+ **Pay the Piper-Urban Dictionary**—Overpaying because not paying the price may result in dire consequences. The moral of the Pied Piper story. When townsfolk didn't pay the piper for ridding the town of rats, the piper kidnapped the town's children. Or, per The Free Dictionary, an idiom coming from the proverb "He who pays the piper calls the tune," implying that the person paying gets to call the shots. Example: Drug lords expect to be in charge of the outcome of their dispensary application if they pay $100,000 to the Mayor.

+ **Racketeering Influenced Corrupt Organizations Act (RICO)**—Originally passed to prosecute the mafia, the RICO Act is now being applied to government organizations that undermine the rule of law, violate rights, are opaque institutions, and lead to lost public resources and weakened national integrity. Example: Appointed officers inside an administrative agency conspiring to use official actions to override a vote of The People.

APPENDIX V RESOURCES

- *Iroquois Confederacy Great Law of Peace*
- *US Declaration of Arbroath*
- *Declaration of Independence*
- *US Constitution*
- John S. Matlin's thesis Political Machines of the 1920s & 30's—Tom Pendergast and the Kansas City Democratic Machine, 2009
- SLO-SPAN.org
  Morro Bay, Ca. 93443
  (805) 772-2715 * agpvideo@agpvideo.com
  Site pioneered by Roscoe Mathieu, Dave Husk, and Steve Mathieu
- Francke, Terry. *Open Meetings in California* (Carmichael, CA. 2015. Californians Aware.)
- Kucinich, Dennis J. *The Division of Light and Power.* (Cleveland, Ohio. 2007. Finney Avenue Books.)
- Robert, Henry M. III. *Robert's Rules of Order, Newly Revised 11th Edition.* (Sarasota, Florida. 2011. Da Capo Press.) New York. 2020. Public Affairs.)
- Steffens, Joseph Lincoln. *The Struggle for Self-Government.* (New York.1968. Johnson Reprint Corporation.),*The Shame of the Cities.* (New York. 1904. Phillips.), *The Autobiography of Lincoln Steffens.* (New York. 1931. Harcourt Brace & Co.)
- Stossel, John. *Give Me a Break: How I exposed Hucksters, Cheaters, And Scam Artists and Became the Scourge of the Liberal Media...*(New York.2004. Harper Perennial.) https://www.amazon.com/Give-Me-Break-Exposed-Hucksters/dp/0060529156

ABOUT THE AUTHOR

A former Mayor, Councilmember, and Planning Commissioner, Debbie Peterson works on both sides of the dais as an advocate for good government.

By the age of 28 Debbie was an award-winning entrepreneur and food manufacturer in Great Britain and has negotiated more than five hundred win-win transactions as a residential real estate broker in California.

Debbie studied journalism and radio-tv, at CSU Fresno, completing a BSc in Communications with a major in Public Relations from the University of Idaho.

Debbie is the author of The HAPPIEST CORRUPTION: *Sleaze, Lies, & Suicide in a California Beach Town,* and the *California Cake & Cookie Cookbook* and was requisitioned by the Scottish Development Agency to write *Great Scotswomen in Business.* Debbie was the Scottish 'Young Business Personality of the Year' before returning to California to raise her son.

She now spends her time writing, speaking, running her real estate company, and skiing and traveling with friends and family.